Economics of
the Black Market

Westview Replica Editions

Economics of the Black Market
S. K. Ray

The black market is a phenomenon that has become increasingly central to the lives of the people in many of the world's economies. In this first serious study of the economics of the black market, Dr. Ray looks in-depth at profiteering, black money, fraud, smuggling, government corruption, and the overall structure of the black market. He explains the effects of the market on prices, inflation, and money supply. He closes with an economic-political strategy to fight what he sees as a growing menace. Though his study is based on the economy of India, the lessons it contains can be applied to many countries where a black-market economy exists.

Dr. S. K. Ray is a senior executive on the Indian Railway Board, specializing in economics and jurisprudence. He has written extensively on the socioeconomic problems in India.

Economics of the Black Market

S. K. Ray

Routledge
Taylor & Francis Group

LONDON AND NEW YORK

First published 1981 by Westview Press

Published 2018 by Routledge
52 Vanderbilt Avenue, New York, NY 10017
2 Park Square, Milton Park, Abingdon, Oxon OX14 4RN

*Routledge is an imprint of the Taylor & Francis Group,
an informa business*

Copyright © 1981 by Taylor & Francis

Library of Congress Cataloging in Publication Data
Ray, S. K.
     Economics of the black market.
     (A Westview replica edition)
     Bibliography: p.
     Includes index.
     1. Black market--India. 2. Black market. 3. Commercial crimes--India.
4. Corruption (in politics)--India. I. Title. II. Series: Westview replica
edition.
HF5482.65.I4R39   330.954'05   81-7589
ISBN 0-86531-149-8   AACR2

ISBN 13: 978-0-367-01863-4 (hbk)
ISBN 13: 978-0-367-16850-6 (pbk)

To my wife

Contents

Tables

Figures

Preface

When way back in 1974, the economics of the black
market and the myriad ways of black money were accepted
as the subject for my thesis for a Ph.D. degree in
Economics, little did we visualise that this would soon
develop into the most topical problem in applied economics in the Indian sub-continent as also in a number of
developing economies of the world.

This, however, did happen. In the background of
the offensive initiated by the central government of
India from mid-1974 and subsequent developments, preg-
nant with possibilities but rather slackening off by
1976, and in the context of the repercussions of certain
subterranean economic forces on the behaviour of the
price spiral, the subject has assumed great importance.

Delving into the subject, through the alleys of the
black market and the dark corridors of corruption and
black money, tax evasion and smuggling, fraud and
misfeasance, I have been struck by the fascinating
character of the study. It was a singular opportunity
to be able to make some yeoman's contribution to an
important aspect of applied economics not adequately
covered as yet.

For, available literature on the subject is meagre.
Plumtre did write a few random articles, in some of the
issues of the Canadian Journal of Economics. Boulding,
incidentally, developed a black market model in his
treatise on marginal analysis while discussing the demand
and supply behaviour consequent upon price regulation and
rationing. A.K. Das Gupta countermanded this model in
his Planning and Economic Growth. Kalechi's analysis on
costs and risks has some relevance to the subject.

There is some analysis on the price spiral in the
Indian situation in the monthly journals of the Reserve
Bank of India Bulletin, a premier monthly forum of
contemporary economic opinion, and the Bank's Annual
Reports on Currency and Finance. Kaldor made some

tentative estimation of black money in India, and this
was further probed by the Direct Taxes Enquiry Committee
in 1970-71, set up by the central government of India.

There have been some official investigations on
corruption in the Indian public life by Committees
headed by Kripalani and later, Santhanam.

And that is about all. The present research therefore has been highly rewarding in the sense that it has
been in the nature of ploughing through acres of virgin
soil.

The method adopted in the research, by the very
nature of things, had to be multi-pronged. The background material, whatever little was available, has been
extensively sifted, studied and made use of, particularly
in the formulation of a theoretical format that did not
exist in the available literature, and therefore had to
be developed almost from the edifice upward.

The ways and means of black market, smuggling, and
such other economic offences, had to be studied principally by means of market surveys and economic investigations independently conducted. This was highly difficult
as the black market is inherently reticent. Questionnaires were developed, and the few guarded replies that
were received elaborately chronicled, but as in neo-
physical sciences, conclusions had to be validated by
indirect and ancillary material backed up by market
intelligence, stock exchange reports and empirical
analyses on price behaviour, money supply and inflation.

Reports and results were studied extensively,
and trends and patterns derived. Advantage was also
taken of official investigations on black money and
corruption, and certain market studies made by institutions like the Indian Council of Applied Economic
Research and opinion polls conducted and answers to
questionnaires tabulated by research organisations like
the Indian Institute of Public Opinion.

Whenever possible, references have been made to
official and non-official documents and publications; in
certain other cases this has not been possible, for
apparent considerations.

A complete bibliography has been drawn up at the
end of the thesis. Permission has been obtained in
respect of references made to a plethora of treatises
and journals during the course of the book, *except of
course, those which should now form an integral part of
the mainstream of knowledge; and in respect of these I
take the opportunity of recording my sincere acknowledge-
ment to the various sources of information.*

Information has been updated to the maximum extent
practicable. Except for certain market-investigations
and behaviour-models briefly referred to or summarised
in subsequent chapters, to make the latter comprehensive,

repetitions have been avoided, even though the subject
dealt with in one chapter does overlap with the subject of
another.

Black market in India, and for that matter in many
other countries, has lately become an integral part of
the economy, and its effects on the economy of the
country and the standard of living of the people have
been not only extensive but highly pestering. It is no
more a craft practised by a few, but has already become
a definite industrial entrepreneurship and business
dealing in which a multitude of persons indulge with
uncanny finesse and organisation.

In conjunction with black money as an ancillary
but nevertheless an extremely potent force, the black
market has become today a major economic evil bedevilling
the economy. The strategies that it deploys, the
currency and produce that it controls, and the socio-
economic repercussions that it fosters, today form a
definite branch of applied economics.

The objectives with which the research was conducted,
and the treatise has been written, can be briefly
summarised as under:

1. To unravel, by investigation and analysis, the
   depth, structure and organisation of the black
   market, its link with black money, their modus
   operandi, and to also assess their social,
   political and economic repercussions on the
   economy and the society. The study has been
   extended to cover certain other allied evils
   like smuggling, corruption, fraud and misfeasance.
2. To make an appraisal, in this context, of the
   price-situation, inflation, money-supply and
   investment-curve, in the Indian economy in
   particular, and to isolate, in the course of
   such an appraisal, the subterranean forces of
   black market, black money and other economic
   offences.
3. To examine the different remedial strategies
   so far evolved and discussed in economic theory
   and practice, in India and abroad, and to make
   an appraisal of their effectiveness in free
   market, mixed and totalitarian economies.
4. To filter the measures best suited to the Indian
   situation and to recommend, in the background
   of our analysis, further remedial strategies
   to combat the forces of the black market, black
   money and other allied economic offences in the
   Indian environment.

Even though the format of the thesis has been drawn
principally against the Indian situation, as an inductive analysis, the concepts and conclusions are applicable, in different degrees, both to developed economies

like the United States and developing economies like the
Indonesian.

Finally, this research has been conducted in my
personal capacity, without in any way affecting my
official duties, and has absolutely nothing to do with
my work as an executive of the Indian Railways.

S. K. Ray
New Delhi, India

Acknowledgments

I have discussed different points of my thesis with
Dr. K.K. Sharma, M.A., Ph.D., D. Litt., a distinguished
author and educationist, Dr. Anil Mukherjee, M.A., D.Litt.,
Professor of Commerce, University of Calcutta, Dr. A.K.
Mathur, M.A., Ph.D., Professor of Economic Development,
Centre of Regional Development, Jawaharlal Nehru Univer-
sity, New Delhi and Dr. Shabhir Ahmed Khan, M.A., Ph.D.,
Professor of Economics, Aligarh University, India.   In
addition, Dr. K.K. Sharma had taken upon himself the
arduous responsibility of editing the manuscript, after
I had revised it for publication as a treatise.   I am
greatly indebted to all of them.

The personal interest and continual encouragement
extended by Mr. Shiv S. Kapur, Director, Operations
Evaluation Department of the World Bank, Washington D.C.,
Mr. P.C. Shukla, Vice-Chairman & Managing Director,
Shipping Corporation of India and Mr. B.R. Nanda, illustrious author and biographer, in my endeavours in
economic journalism over two decades, had finally
culminated in the writing of the thesis and the treatise
on the black market and the parallel economy, and no
simple acknowledgment can repay their debt.   In fact,
it is their constant encouragement that had prompted me
to start on my second book, Economics of the Third
World.

I am also grateful to Dr. Hannan Ezekiel, Editor,
Economic Times, Bombay, Mr. V. Balasubramanian, Editor,
Eastern Economist, New Delhi, Mr. A.K. Dutta, Editor,
Management Accountant, Calcutta, Mr. C.P. Raghavan,
Editor, Financial Express, Bombay, and Dr. D.K. Rangnekar,
Editor, Business Stadard, Calcutta, for giving permis-
sion to profusely draw in the course of my treatise
from portions of my own articles published in their
esteemed papers and journals during the last two decades.
I am also indebted to my friends from the press,
acquired from the days I was Public Relations Officer

xxii

of the Northern Railway at New Delhi, for allowing me
the use of many of their files of press-clippings.

I am grateful to Mr. S. Sivaraman, Librarian, Indian
Railway Board and Mr. S.R. Shah, formerly Secretary to
General Manager, Northern Railway at New Delhi, for not
only allowing me extensive use of their libraries, but
also obtaining for my use books, journals, reports, acts,
documents and periodicals from different other libraries
in the Indian capital attached to Universities, Chambers
of Commerce, Ministries and Public Institutions like the
Indian Council of Applied Economic Research and the
Institute of Public Opinion, New Delhi. Being a senior
government executive myself, and having conducted the
research without any study leave, I could hardly have
been able to do the requisite library-work but for the
unstinted help of these two friends.

I am obliged to Messrs K.K. Puri, O.P. Narula,
H.S. Rana, Ram Prashad, Mahendra Kumar, J.R. Sardana
and Ms. H. Batra for attending to typing, calligraphy,
draftsmanship and organisational details of my treatise.
I am grateful to Mr. A.P. Ramannan, an executive of the
Indian Railways, for his assistance in the preparation
of the index.

I am indebted to Mr. Leon H. Miller, Senior
Economist in the World Bank, Washington D.C. and
Ms. Lynne C. Rienner, Associate Publisher, Westview
Press, Boulder, USA, for their abiding interest and
valuable counsel in the editing and publication of the
manuscript.

Finally, I have a debt to my wife, Ruchira Ray,
M.A., M.Ed., and a Kailashvati Gold Medalist of Lucknow
University, India. It is only because she was able to
bear with a husband who has been working in the office
during the day and poring over books and papers in the
morning and night, Sundays and holidays inclusive, over
a year and a half, and also attended to the studies
and upbringing of our two sons all by herself, that
I have been able to complete the research and write the
treatise.

                                        S.K.R.

Economics of
the Black Market

1

An Introduction to the Concept

Discussion on black marketing from the viewpoint of an economic analyst is rare. But for Plumtre's <u>Theory of the Black Market</u>[1], we can scarcely think of another important study on the subject. This is somewhat paradoxical, particularly for economic scholarship in a number of developing countries, where the forces of the black market now wield partial suzerainty not only over the procurement and distribution systems, but also on currency-circulation and the national liquidity-situation.

It is often said that the black market as a trend of business entrepreneurship does not as yet come within the purview of economic generalisations, and that it is only an abnormal and short-period exception to the general economic laws.

In most countries governed by free economy, and more than most in a mixed economy like the Indian, nothing could be farther from the truth. Black market during the last few decades has been a way of life. Its effect on the economic life of the people has become far-reaching and highly pestering. Black marketing in the economy is no more confined to a few clandestine trade deals, but has already become a well-defined form of business dealing and industrial entrepreneurship.

In conjunction with black money, as an ancillary but nevertheless a very potent force, the black market, in the Indian sub-continent for instance, has become a hydra-headed economic monster. The strategies that it deploys, the currency and produce that it controls, and the socio-economic repercussions that it fosters, today form a definite branch of economics.

<u>The price spiral</u>

The general price index of wholesale prices in India (base 1961-62 = 100) increased in the early 'seventies by 154 percent showing a compound rate of increase of a little over 8 percent a year. In the subsequent years, the increase has been even more phenomenal. Except for a brief pause in 1975, the

1

inflationary pressure on prices has been relentless,
continual and unabated.

Sugar prices went up by a colossal 126.8 percent
in the past year while those of potatoes rose by as much
as 69.9 percent, according to the latest official
analysis. The analysis covered 21 items, including rice
and wheat, that showed a significant rise in price
during the latest twelve months and, ominously, most of
these have been food items.[2]

The inflationary fever of the price level has been
conditioned by a multiplicity of different factors;
variations and failures in agricultural production,
large-scale imports of foodgrains, consequences of wars
and refugee rehabilitation and, finally, deficit
financing had all their roles to play; but a major
guiding factor that has all the while been influencing
the price level has been the forces unleashed by black
market and black money.

The position of the national economy was analysed
in the Annual Report of the Reserve Bank of India for
1973-74. The Report brought out that the increase in
aggregate output in 1973-74 was higher than in the
previous year. Yet this did not result in a slowing
down in the rise of prices. In fact, the Reserve Bank of
India in this report had cautioned the government of the
danger of a hyperinflation and a run-away price-spiral,
if deterrent and comprehensive measures were not
enforced. These counsels of caution have been reiterated
in the Bank's Annual Report for 1979-80.[3]

The behaviour pattern of the price spiral has been
widely governed by hoarding, money-jumping, speculation,
stock-piling and underhand procurement and release of
commodities under the economic forces of the black market,
substantially governed by black money.

In this background, it has to be accepted
unhesitatingly that black market today has become a
force to reckon with and certainly deserves a complete
socio-economic investigation.

The economic laws

And, reverting back to the assertion that the black
market as yet does not come within the purview of economic
laws, it is today debatable how far can we rely any longer
on these time-honoured economic laws as to their
perfection and accuracy under all circumstances.

Economic laws hold good for aggregates and not for
individual instances. They set forth the average
relationship between phenomena. They are approximations
or tendencies.[4] We would, therefore, believe that
whenever business dealing and industrial entrepreneurship
in any particular direction assume sufficient importance
as to their nature and extent, there should be special
examination of the same in applied economics.

In economics as a humanitarian science, changes
in the socio-economic phenomena, or in relevant
substantive or peripheral economic laws, have been duly
reckoned with, and adjustments made in the ideation of
the economic theory and the ramification of planning
and development.

Contrary to the assumption in certain quarters,
economics, in the humanitarian sense, from Marshall to
Kuznets, has been based on a continuous process of
exploration, and let us admit, has made room for
necessary adjustments in the theory as also in the
dynamics of development.

It would be fallacious to think that once an
economic law was given, it was perfect and that it would
determine all future developments based on it, or in
pursuance of it. The law itself was subjected to
continuous research and would often give way to new
findings or explorations. It has not been, as it were
sometimes presumed, that the law was supreme, once and
for all.[5] (Cf. annexure 1).

Pigovian simplification

To give an example of such a phenomenon, we may
refer to Pigou. In his Theory of Unemployment, Pigou
theorised that, with perfectly free competition amongst
working people and labour perfectly mobile, the nature
of relationship (between the real wage-rates for which
people would stipulate and the demand function for
labour) would be very simple; there would always be
a strong tendency for wage rates to be so related to
demand that everybody was employed. Hence, Pigou
concluded, in stable conditions everyone would actually
be employed.[6]

In terms of an exposition of a given economic law,
there is no doubt that such a simplification of the
realities as Pigou elected to adopt, in order to fit his
premises to a theory, does not stand the test of today's
economic behaviour. Pigou propounded this theory by
taking recourse to mathematical presumptions, and
preferred to ignore a large number of variables - not
that he was not vaguely aware of some of the possible
variables.[7]

That is what happens when an economic law, once
formulated, is idealised as a conformist norm of economic
behaviour. It becomes so rigid that it ceases to be
applicable in actual fiscal, developmental, planning
and monetary policies.

Both in terms of further explorations on the given
economic laws, and as a definitive behaviour-pattern of
economic forces, black marketing, or more appropriately,
the black market, certainly deserves an analysis in
depth regarding its nature, extent and socio-economic
repercussions. Such an analysis, based on an

investigation of the Indian situation, if conducted on a pragmatic, didactic and realistic way, would prove to be highly utilitarian as an econo-sociological exploration.

A definition

What, after all, is the black market ? When by (artificial) manipulation of the economic forces of demand and supply, of both currency and produce (or either), the trade or the industry (or both) create an artificial situation of scarcity or glut, and in the process amass huge returns on their investments, by what in chapter 2 we shall discuss as profiteering, we have a black market situation.

A number of neo-classical economists wrote about social prerogative and individual prerogative among businessmen. It was observed that by moral pursuasion, businessmen should be made inclined to socialize their business endeavours. Clay, in his Economics for the General Reader, advised businessmen and entrepreneurs that it was to society's interest that they should reflect on and realise the social effects of their private actions. A reflection of these ideas is available in the latest trend of a section of the econo-political analysis of the Indian price spiral.

These are, as far as they go, no more than eulogies. And despite this eulogy of a social approach to business, industrial or business enterprise has manifested itself in no inconsequential measure in unsocial, individualistic and anti-people tendencies.

The Indian situation, for instance, is replete with illustrative instances of such phenomena. It has been experienced, particularly during the last two decades, how legitimate speculation has been reduced to illegitimate gambling, stock of merchandise (particularly inelastics) has been hoarded in order to create artificial scarcity, and prices have been hiked by sterilising the age-old economic laws. By artificial manipulation of consumption-propensity and thereby affecting the level of demand, the spiral-potential of prices has been tapped by entrepreneurs and businessmen to accumulate huge margins on their turnover.

The situation is no different and, if at all, the difference is only of degrees, in respect of a number of other countries selected at random, with developed as also developing economies, that the present author had occasion to survey.

A theory

A theory of the black market may take shape in the trail of the Joan Robinson-Chamberlin-Triffin sequence of the theories of monopolistic competition. Before the depression of the 'thirties, it was generally believed by economists that available economic theory was able to analyse the prevalent patterns of industrial entrepreneurship which were either perfectly competitive or monopolistic.

As to the relative importance they attached to these two groups of industries, there has been wide divergence of both appraoch and opinion. Surprisingly enough, however, they adopted more or less an uniform tenor of economic analysis. From this, however, it should not be concluded that "the details of the analytical system were, or were thought to be, definitive. As a matter of fact, certain portions of the system, such as duopoly, admittedly were (and are) in wretched shape".

At this point came the works of a number of economists like Joan Robinson and Chamberlin, demanding a radical orientation of approach and outlook. A good part of such literature, fundamentally, was no real break-away from the tradition of neo-classical economics; indeed, as was said, it contained too uncritical an acceptance of the substantive context of orthodoxy.

But Chamberlin's magnum opus, The Theory of Monopolistic Competition, was, in spite of some contemporaneous criticism, revolutionary in character. Indeed, it was Chamberlin who brought home to us the point that "no simple dichotomy does justice to the rich variety of industrial organisation".

Chamberlin

Chamberlin felt that different types of industrial entrepreneurship including duopoly, monopsony, oligopsony and increasingly imperfect competition were too intricate to be analysed adequately by the available tenets of theory. Available theory was of the patent type and failed to ramify the intricacies of a growingly complex entrepreneural set-up.

Chamberlin investigated the position in depth. He accepted that there were (a very few) industries that closely resembled those studied by the economists of perfect competition and that there were (perhaps more) concerns that partook of the nature of monopoly as this concept was used in neo-classical economies. But vastly more often, Chamberlin added, the trade and the industrial firms displayed a mixture of insulation from competitors or consumers.

It has been our experience, more than most in an heterogeneous economic situation like the Indian, that such insulation is frequently established by real or fancied product-differentiation, by playing-up or scaling down the forces of demand and supply, thereby exerting subterranean pressures on liquidity-preference or consumption-propensity, or more often by straight-jacket hoarding or similar other devices of the black market. As a result, there are important, in fact, typical, phenomena, which cannot be explained, or can be explained with serious error, if economic reality is forced into a rigid neo-classical theory.[8]

Here comes the recurrent question as to whether the
black market should be considered such a typical phenomenon. As has been examined in the foregoing paragraphs,
and perhaps firmly established throughout the present
treatise, there is no good reason as to why should it not
be. Here, of course, it is obvious that an inductive
approach is expected to yield better results and, come
to think of it, there is nothing wrong with an inductive
analysis.

Concrete cases

Here one may sound a rational note. To a considerable extent, a substantial proportion of neo-classical
economics was built on an edifice of a whole gamut of
simplified assumptions, rather arbitrarily made to
circumvent the explanation of economic variables, and
the process unduly extended towards the examination of
the general economic phenomena. Our theory, therefore,
as advised by economists like Chamberlin, Triffin et al,
will recognise the richness and variety of all concrete
cases, and tackle each problem with due deference. More
advantage will be taken of all relevant factual information and less reliance will be placed on a mere resort
to the pass-key of general theoretical assumptions.[9]

In trying to establish a theory of the black market,
from an analysis of demand and supply in a market
governed by imperfect competition, one has to reckon
with a few pitfalls of an excessively simplified
theorisation.

Mere excess of demand over supply, leading to higher
and higher prices and profits, is not necessarily black
marketing. This can happen in open markets also.
Secondly, a stage comes when the state or law intervenes
to protect social interests against private interests.

The state legislates regarding fair prices, standa-
rdised production and cooperative distribution. Getting
over these laws and practices by entrepreneurs leads to
the eruption, existence and proliferation of the black
market. Instances of these phenomena will be liberally
given from the Indian situation in appropriate places in
subsequent chapters.

One remembers that with a sudden breakdown in the
sense of values in the trail of the second world war,
correlated with scarcity conditions of a war economy,
black marketing became a notoriously popular practice
with the Indian trade.[10]

War and post-war inflation, and a continuously
spiralling price-level (consequent upon the developmental investments based on financing by budgetary gaps
and international borrowings), gave the Indian black
market an unfortunate shot in the arm.

Together with it worked the growing forces and

influences of the black money. As it will be discussed
later in the study, in chapters 3, 5 and 6, this has now
become inter-linked, even coextensive, with the black
market. It has thereby grown out of its infancy and has
grown in its structure so as to rule or govern the forces
of economy in a substantial measure.[11]
    As to whether it has become an alternative, or a
parallel economy, is a separate subject altogether,[12]
and will be discussed as such in the proper sequence.

Objectives

    After having determined the nature of the concept,
and the need and method of investigations, it is the
purpose of this study to unravel, by investigation and
analysis, the depth, structure, organisation and
objectives of the black market, with particular reference
to the Indian situation, its possible link with black
money, their modus operandi, and also assess their social,
political and economic repercussions on the economy and
the society.
    It is also the objective of the present study to
examine the possible remedial strategies so far evolved
and discussed in economic theory and practice, in India
and abroad, and to make an appraisal of their effectiveness in free market and totalitarian economies. It is
the intention, finally, to recommend, in the background
of such an appraisal, a remedial strategy for combating
the forces of the black market, in a free market economy,
with particular relevance to the Indian situation.

NOTES

    1. A.F.W. Plumtre - Theory of the Black Market;
Canadian Journal of Economics & Political Science; 1947.
    2. K.K. Sharma - The Statesman, New Delhi;
August 21, 1980.
        S.K. Ray - Economic Growth Prospects; Financial
Express, Bombay; January 3, 5 & 6, 1981.
    3. Annual Reports on Currency and Banking, 1973-74
and 1979-80; Reserve Bank of India.
    4. Hansen - Principles of Political Economy.
        Clay - Economics for the General Reader.
    5. S.K. Ray - Recent Trends in Fundamental
Economics; Eastern Economist; New Delhi, August 15, 1975.
        S.K. Ray - Should Economics Play Second Fiddle?;
Financial Express, Bombay, December 20, 1980. The
article is reproduced as annexure 1.
    6. A.C. Pigou - Theory of Unemployment.
    7. J.M. Keynes - General Theory of Employment,
Interest and Money (1951); Appendix to Chapter 19;
Macmillan and Company, London.
    8. Chamberlin - Economics of Monopolistic Competi-
tion; Oxford University Press, London.

8

9. Chamberlin - Ibid.
Triffin - <u>Monopolistic Competition and General Equilibrium Theory</u>.
10. S.K. Ray - <u>Profiteering, An Economic Analysis</u>; Eastern Economist; New Delhi, October 17, 1975.
11. <u>Final Report of Direct Taxes Enquiry Committee</u>, Government of India, 1971.
12. S.K. Ray - <u>Emergence and Proliferation of Black Money</u>; Economic Times, Bombay, May 3 & 4, 1978.

2

Economics of Profiteering

From a study of the price index in July 1974 for the Delhi metropolis, it is found that despite fairly satisfactory market arrivals and partial rationing, the prices of <u>cereals</u> alone soared by 47.3 percent in the Delhi markets within the course of a month (Table 2.1).

Similarly for <u>soap,</u> a representative consumer goods item, prices over three months increased by over 150 percent, despite an actual increase by about 17 percent in their production in the country and nearly 20 percent increase in the total ex-factory releases for the Delhi metropolitan area (Table 2.2).

Compared to this, there has been no tangible change in the demographic curve for the capital or shift in the consumers' surplus curve for these commodities, mostly inelastic, during the previous six months to a year.

An analysis of the supply and demand curves in the black market in India is the best ready reckoner of its objectives. The edifice of the Indian black market is principally what economists call <u>unsatisfied demand.</u> As to how this is achieved is a separate matter, and will be discussed in subsequent chapters. Anyway, one thing is almost axiomatic. As a result of the black market manoeuvres, the black market supply curve will lie to the left of the normal supply curve.[1]

<u>Supply flows</u>

Black marketing, it has to be appreciated, is no freshman's job. Like the artistry of a black magician, manoeuvres of the black marketeer also require considerable skill and understanding of the market situation, in relation to both credit and liquidity as also supply and demand.

While this is one aspect of the matter, another equally important aspect is that black marketing, by the very nature of things, contains considerable elements of risk and cost, particularly in the efforts by the

10

Table 2.1
Arrival and price behaviour of cereals in Delhi Market

July 1974   Base - Last week of June 1974

Week	Percentage increase/ decrease in market arrivals	Percentage increase/ decrease in price spiral
First week	+ 9.11	+ 42.6
Second week	+ 21.2	+ 51.1
Third week	- 0.3	+ 59.3
Fourth week	+ 17.0	+ 41.2

Source:

1. Bulletin on Food Statistics, Ministry of Food &
       Agriculture, Government of India.
    2. Indian Agriculture in Brief, Ministry of Food &
       Agriculture, Government of India.
    3. The Statesman, New Delhi; issues of June &
       July 1974.
    4. Economic Times, Bombay; issues of June &
       July 1974.

Table 2.2
Price behaviour vis-à-vis market arrivals of soap
in Delhi Metropolitan market

Base - April 1974

Month of 1974	Percentage increase/ decrease in overall recorded production in the country	Percentage increase/ decrease in arrivals in Delhi metropolitan markets	Percentage increase/ decrease in price spiral in Delhi metropolitan markets
May	+ 0.29	+ 5.30	+ 172.4
June	+ 23.10	+ 32.60	+ 125.2
July	+ 17.60	+ 29.90	+ 149.5

Source:

    1. Indian Agriculture in Brief, Ministry of Food
       & Agriculture, Government of India.
    2. Yojana, Delhi; Fortnightly issues;
       January to August 1974.
    3. The Statesman, New Delhi; issues of April to
       July 1974.

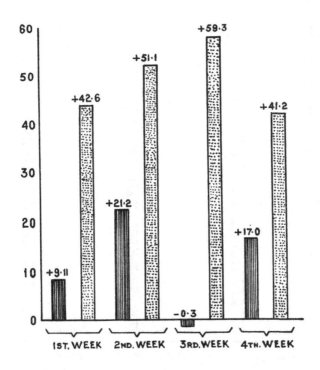

% INCREASE/DECREASE IN MARKET ARRIVALS

% INCREASE/DECREASE IN PRICE SPIRAL

BASE-LAST WEEK OF JUNE, 1974.

MARKET ARRIVALS AND PRICE BEHAVIOUR OF
CEREALS IN DELHI MARKET DURING JULY, 1974.

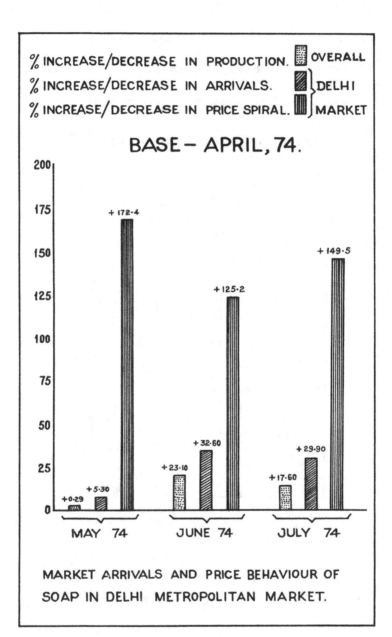

% INCREASE/DECREASE IN PRODUCTION. OVERALL
% INCREASE/DECREASE IN ARRIVALS. DELHI
% INCREASE/DECREASE IN PRICE SPIRAL. MARKET

BASE – APRIL, 74.

MARKET ARRIVALS AND PRICE BEHAVIOUR OF
SOAP IN DELHI METROPOLITAN MARKET.

manipulators to hijack the price spiral, and while on the errand of profiteering.

It is in view of this element of cost and risk that black market suppliers will not be willing to release to the market as much quantity of any commodity, which they have <u>cornered</u>, as would happen when market conditions are free from the strategies of the black market.

On the contrary, what will normally happen in the black market is that a higher price level, artificially pegged up, will <u>chase</u> a restricted supply, most of the time. Rather very occasionally may there be a comparative price stabilisation only at the height of a plateau, <u>provided</u> that gives the maximum turnover of black market profits.

If at a higher level of price, it so happens that the accounting of the black-marketeer indicates that the next turnover will fetch him more profit, if a relatively higher supply is made, only then he would do so. Not normally otherwise. Under normal black market conditions, because of higher costs, only a higher price will prompt higher supply than before.[2]

The greater the overhead on black marketing, the steeper will be the rise of the supply curve in the black market, to spread out the overhead.

<u>Demand curve</u>

As in case of a supply curve, it is similarly possible to postulate, what we may call, a demand curve under black market conditions. Let us take the case of <u>sugar</u>, a <u>compromise</u> between elastic and inelastic commodities, for the Delhi market. For the purpose of the present investigation, the market behaviour for this commodity during May to July 1974 was studied.[3] (Table 2.3).

There was an increase in the ex-factory release of sugar for the Delhi metropolitan area by approximately 19.7 percent. There was, however, a shortfall in the supply of sugar in the <u>open market</u>. In the Delhi metropolitan markets, the rise in prices had ranged between 32 and 49 percent. The base price has been taken to be what ruled in the market during April 1973, a <u>comparatively</u> stable month for prices.

The fact that there was partial rationing in sugar enabled the black market operators to rule the roost. For one thing, a very large number of the population in Delhi are not ration-card holders. Secondly, (even though no proper study has yet been made about the extent of <u>ghost</u> cards in Delhi metropolitan area), it is believed that about 30 percent of the sugar released through rationing goes to <u>ghost</u>-card holders amongst <u>halwais</u> and hoteliers.

Thirdly, the circumscribed releases through rationing only tended to whet the demands for this

Table 2.3
Supply and Price Behaviour of Sugar in Delhi
Metropolitan Market

Period May to July 1974   Base - April 1973

Month of 1974	Percentage increase or decrease for Delhi metropolitan market (ex-factory releases)	Arrival in the open market	Percentage increase/ decrease in the open market prices	Percentage increase in the black market prices
May	+ 7.3	- 3.8	+ 2.5	+ 32.8
June	+ 11.2	- 6.5	+ 2.5	+ 41.2
July	- 1.1	- 21.5	+ 2.7	+ 49.1

Source:

1. Financial Express, New Delhi; market information in all issues from May 1 to July 31, 1974, as compared to similar information from April 1 to 30, 1973.
2. Economic Times, Bombay; as in item 1 above.
3. Margin, New Delhi,Quarterly Journal of the National Council of Applied Economic Research, 1973 & 1974.

commodity in the open market, which was almost exclusively outside the spheres of limited rationing, and within nearly complete control of the black market.

The behaviour pattern of demand has been made to fluctuate by the black market operators by spreading rumours about the state of supply, both through rationing and otherwise. Towards the end of May 1974, when the state of demand for sugar tended to stagnate, both in the Delhi metropolis and elsewhere in the country, because of an improvement in supply, feverish rumours were made afloat about impending nationalisation of the sugar industry, a probable decision to increase export of sugar at double the current level and even a possible hike in the levy price of sugar to be allowed by government within a short period.[4]

From this investigation, three conclusions emerge. First, the demand and supply functions are not independent of extraneous forces (or pressure strategies) as it should normally happen in a free market economy, and the ruling price at any point of time is not necessarily the consequence of the market stabilizer as this concept is commonly understood, and as are often attempted through naive measures which may not strike at the roots of the

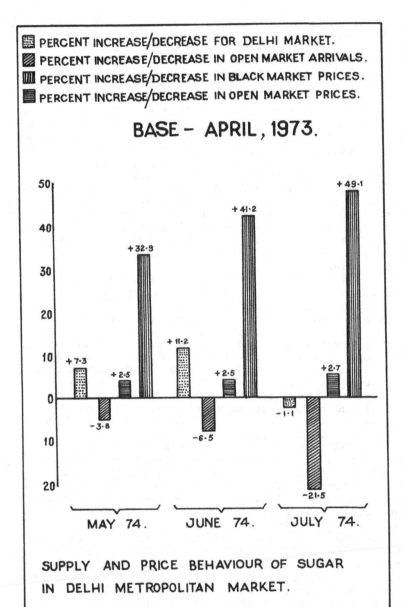

PERCENT INCREASE/DECREASE FOR DELHI MARKET.
PERCENT INCREASE/DECREASE IN OPEN MARKET ARRIVALS.
PERCENT INCREASE/DECREASE IN BLACK MARKET PRICES.
PERCENT INCREASE/DECREASE IN OPEN MARKET PRICES.

BASE – APRIL, 1973.

SUPPLY AND PRICE BEHAVIOUR OF SUGAR IN DELHI METROPOLITAN MARKET.

complicated market phenomenon.

Similarly, the price spiral in the black market is always conditioned by artificial manipulation of either demand or supply or both, in order to attain the maximum attainable margin between costs and turnover.

As a result, (as indicated while introducing the concept of black market supply flows earlier in this chapter), the price curve in black market, after some time, may be on a plateau, if that would yield such a margin. But usually more often, because of the multiplicity in the number of operators in the black market, a fluctuating price curve with a generally upward slant would generally rule the market conditions.

Finally, the end of the black market is neither the economic function of productivity and growth, nor the social or welfare function of an equitable distribution of the gross national product; but is, all the while, the rather pedestrian function of maximisation of the net return. In other words, the objective of the black market, in economic abbreviation, is profiteering.

Profiteering

Profiteering, as an economic function, has to be understood as a concept distinct from profit. Profit, as enunciated by Pigou, is a particular species of monetary gain, monetary gain secured in a particular way ... To make a profit, in the sense here relevant, implies performing a middleman's or an entrepreneur's function, hiring the services of other men or buying goods from other men, and selling the product or the services or the goods and obtaining, as a reward, the difference between outlay and receipt.[5]

If the difference is made to exceed a socially acceptable limit, and that by questionable methods, it is a case of profiteering.

Way back in the first chapter, we had established that we have to shelve, for the purpose of a realistic economic analysis, the principles governing perfect market competition, and have to reckon with the forces of imperfect competition, duopoly monopsony and oligopoly, monopolistic competition and the black market.

Assumptions invalid

Before we go to analyse the economic process of profit-making, and in that context, the theory of profit-optimisation, and finally profiteering, it is necessary to appreciate that it would no longer suffice to assume merely that demand and supply curves exist, that some are elastic and some inelastic, or that some rise and fall... If we do not do so, we will be reducing the study of economic phenomena of today's market situation to the simplicity of a middle-form class-room.

The assumptions of perfect competition, on which

much of supply and demand analysis is based, must also
be scrutinised. Boulding has firmly concluded that in
today's economic situation perfect competition has ceased
to exist except in the imagination of economists... Over
large spheres of economic life other and more complicated
systems of relationships are of importance and that these
only are relevant in any pragmatic study of market
behaviour.[6]

Let us first indicate the principle of profit-
making process in a market of imperfect competition.
Very briefly, the profit-making process under imperfect
market conditions is determined by what they call the
dynamics of a marketer. Boulding explained that in the
marketing of a product or a service, the larger the
swings in a profitable succession of transformation of
the product or the service (or in short, the investment),
the greater the total profit.[7]

But this is not all. The play of these swings is
restricted, or even determined, by the nature and extent
of market-imperfection and the presence and delineation
of risks and uncertainty.

Profit optimisation

According to the theory of profit optimisation, the
marginal conditions of the market will lead to optimisation of production in relation to its total marketable
cost component, so that, what we may call, maximum
average revenue for minimum average cost is achieved. In
any case, this will be the objective of the economic
functions of a marketer under imperfect competition, in
his endeavour for optimisation of profit.[8]

A theory of the black market can take off from the
point of profit optimisation. The changeover is vastly
or only in relation to the changeover of the objective
from profit optimisation to profit maximisation, by any
or all means.

Profit maximisation, or profiteering, will be
conditioned by the principle of increasing risk and
uncertainty, as Kalechi calls it. With the increase in
the potential of risks on the investment coefficient,
the profits will increase or decrease mostly on the
extent of risk-taking.[9]

In the end, an element of speculation will permeate
the trading process, as imperfection increases, and with
the entry of black market conditions, this will gradually
generate into cornering or even unlawful speculation in
merchandise.

The general feeling that profiteering is possible
only at the height of a boom is incorrect. There are,
as is the experience today, means to attain this even at
the depth of a slump, and in the different stages in
between the two antipodal phenomena.

The necessary margin between cost and price required
for profiteering may be kept by artificial contraction of
supply in relation to demand, through hoarding or sealed
production, or by tapping the inflationary fever of
purchasing power, through effective manipulation of
supply or liquidity or both. In either case, there is
an artificial scarcity of supply in relation to both
consumption propensity (demand) and liquidity preference
(purchasing power).

What ensues is a serious gap between the normal
demand and the black market supply, or in other words,
unchanged demand chasing after a much contracted supply.
In more senses than one, this gap accounts for the
levels of profiteering in the black market, and is a
very common experience in the market situation in the
Indian sub-continent.

What is more, the black market demand curve may rise
even more sharply than expected and cross the regular
demand curve. This is because the operators in the black
market either very well know or sometimes even foster the
basic human frailty of aspiring for a commodity that is
not easily attainable. For economic inelastics, like
rice, cooking oil or wheat, this is achieved with little
manoeuvring. In such a case, the black market price may
well be much higher.[10]

An earmark of the black market, often, therefore, is
a pushed-up price level. But from an imperfect-market
study, one would say, a rapidly fluctuating price level
is more important to a black marketeer; for, this enables
him to initiate price gambols and, not infrequently to
artificially play up consumption-propensity or liquidity-
preference. All these, in a straight-jacket pattern, add
to his capacity for profiteering.

A fluctuating price-level under black market
conditions may be attained, as is often done, by spreading rumours as to the state of supply or, more frequently
of demand; or more probably by buying or selling in
direct opposition to the black marketeers' forecast of
price movement in order to thrust the price spiral upward
or downward. Hoarding may be yet another convenient but
simple means to achieve this.
An investigation

The mechanism of profiteering under black market
conditions in India can be studied by an economic
investigation on the behaviour pattern of the prices,
demand and supply of vegetable oil in the Delhi markets
during May to July, 1974. (Table 2.4)

The market arrivals in vegetable oil in the beginning was good. Adequate quantity was also being available
in the market. Overnight there was a rumour, spread
across all the markets of Delhi, that there were going
to be raids conducted by the Delhi Civil Administration

Table 2.4
Behaviour pattern of supply, demand and prices of
vegetable oil in Delhi Metropolitan market

Period May to July 1974   Base - April 1973

Month of 1974	Supply		Demand	Prices	
	Percentage increase in ex-factory releases for Delhi metropo-litan area	Actual arri-vals in the open market, percent-age to total supply	Perce-ntage of black market demand to total demand	Percent-age increase/ decrease in the open market, including partial rationing and fair price shops	Percentage increase in the black market
May	+ 3.8	39	56	+ 2.8	+ 52.5
June	+ 2.7	41	34	+ 2.9	+ 59.3
July	+ 5.1	47.5	31	+ 3.2	+ 73.1

Source:

> The study has been made, based mainly on market reports on the supply, demand and price behaviour of vegetable oil (hydrogenated cooking oil) in the Delhi market, as reported by the literature of a reputed stock brokers' firm and market intelligence reported for this period in the pages of commerce and finance in Financial Express and the Statesman, Delhi and Economic Times, Bombay.

on important consumable commodities, including vegetable oil, and the latter just went underground. The raids, however, were (and actually planned to be) conducted on cereals. But the supply of vegetable oil which had gone underground did not surface, except at higher black market prices, on the sly, as a sort of a favour to regular customers.

The government procured a large quantity and stocked them in the super markets and cooperative stores for supply at a reasonable price to be issued to ration-card holders, in order to inject a sobering effect on the market. What ensued is a common experience in many countries.

The black market operators engaged a large number of trip-boys and cornered bulk of supply, and hoarded the same in the black market. The same phenomenon of sealed supply, regulated release, high black market price,

20

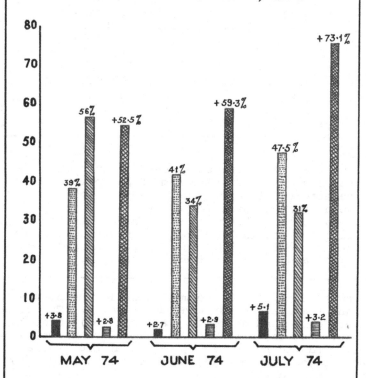

SUPPLY, % INCREASE/DECREASE FOR DELHI MARKET
ACTUAL ARRIVALS IN OPEN MARKET, % TO TOTAL SUPPLY.
% OF BLACK MARKET DEMAND TO TOTAL DEMAND.
PRICES, % INCREASE/DECREASE IN OPEN MARKET.
PRICES, % INCREASE/DECREASE IN BLACK MARKET.

BASE – APRIL, 1973.

BEHAVIOUR PATTERN OF SUPPLY, DEMAND AND PRICES
OF VEGETABLE OIL IN DELHI METROPOLITAN MARKET.

unsatisfied demand, still higher price, more contracted supply and the gradual effect of the multiplier and the accelerator started to interact.

As a result, the operators in the black market made merry with the cornered supply and made fabulous profits.

Towards the middle of June 1974, there was yet another development which further aided the black marketeer. They had already apparently cornered a large quantity of the product when factories producing vegetable oil started regulating, and gradually, closing down their production, in view of a duty imposed by the government on a major ingredient.

This was much to the advantage of the black market operators, and they made the most of it. The play of prices in the South Delhi markets was marked over this period (fortnightly averages) like the surface of a sea hit by a hurricane.

Estimate of profiteering

According to our estimate, for the quarter-year under review, against an approximate 17.2 percent increase in the ex-factory releases of vegetable oil for the entire Delhi markets, the average price rise in the black market has been around 85 percent, total consumption went down by 11 percent, the black-marketeer's profit went up by more than 150 percent.

Agreed that these are approximations and cannot be fairly accurate, mainly in view of the difficulties in collecting market intelligence regarding black market purchases and turnover; but these are indicative of the range of profiteering in the black market on vegetable oil and, for that matter, on other commodities.

In today's market conditions, the black market operators in vegetable oil have been able to cash on any development in the market. There are mainly two reasons for this. First, in the Delhi metropolitan area, the availability of cooking oil (mustard, coconut etc.) has also been unsatisfactory, and the supply (and price) of pure ghee (cooking butter) has remained beyond the means of over eighty-five percent of the population.

Secondly, (a strange psychological consumer-behaviour), the greatest number of people seem to have taken to vegetable oil as a substitute for pure ghee rather than as a substitute for cooking oil. Any dislocation in the market has consistently helped, for the period under study, the operators in the black market very substantially in achieving price hikes, cornering and hoarding of the commodity, and in downright profiteering.

Profiteering is not only the principal, but the sole objective for the black market operators in India today. Profiteering in the black market, as an economic phenomenon, is achieved by sponsoring an interaction in

the curves of (unsatisfied) demand and (restricted)
supply, with first a multiplier and then an accelerator
effect, aided further by a multiplicity of the commodity
and the wave of the price spiral.[11]

While the analysis has been based on market-
investigations made in India, the situation is typical
of similar market-conditions anywhere else in the world.
Subject to shifts in the emphasis exerted by individual
variables, the analysis can be taken, mutatis mutandis,
as the picture of a representative economic phenomenon
in the world today.

NOTES

1. S.K. Ray - Profiteering, An Economic Analysis;
Eastern Economist; New Delhi, October 17, 1975.
S.K. Ray - The Profiteering Curve; Financial
Express, Bombay, May 9, 1977.
2. Boulding - Economic Analysis (1955); Hamish
Hamilton, London.
3. S.K. Ray - Economics of Profit; Business
Standard, Calcutta, February 17 & 18, 1978.
4. The analysis on sugar in Delhi metropolitan
market can be represented in a graphical pattern, not
only to illustrate the behaviour pattern in the black
market of sugar, but also the effects of partial control
and rationing and measures taken by the government to
stabilise the market in sugar. We can draw our graph,
as Boulding did, on the basis of what he called the
supply and demand curve analysis. (Boulding - Economic
Analysis).
5. A.C. Pigou - Socialism Versus Capitalism.
6. Boulding - Economic Analysis.
7. Ibid.
8. Ibid.
9. Kalechi - The Principle of Economic Risk;
Economica, November 1937.
10. S.K. Ray - Profiteering, An Economic Analysis;
Eastern Economist; New Delhi, October 17, 1975.
11. S.K. Ray - The Profiteering Curve; Financial
Express, Bombay, May 9, 1977.

3

The Parallel Economy

Nicholas Kaldor from Cambridge came to India in
1955. At a seminar he attended at Pune, near Bombay,
and later during his visit to New Delhi, he had extensive
discussions on the extent of money circulating in the
country that was eluding the network of taxation.

Back to Cambridge, Kaldor continued his research
on the subject. The following year he produced a volume
entitled <u>Indian Tax Reforms</u>. It was in this treatise that
an attempt was made, seriously for the first time, to
compute the extensiveness of <u>black money</u> circulating in
the Indian system.

Kaldor was conscious about the sensitivity of his
calculations and for that matter of the margin of
probability in any such calculations. Besides, Kaldor
made his calculations in the background of the possible
magnitude of evasion of public finance through a comparison of national income estimates to income tax assessments.

The method involved many <u>assumptions</u> regarding the
components of national income and also had to reckon
with the inadequacy of information on estimates of tax
evasion, particularly in what may be called the
disorganised sector of public finance. Here obviously
he was referring <u>inter alia</u> to black money and black
market. Kaldor himself postulated that the estimates
were tentative and must be interpreted with caution.[1]

<u>Kaldor's estimate</u>

Nevertheless, an analysis of the margin between
Kaldor's estimate of assessable income and the actual
figures of assessed income did provide an indication of
the order of evasion, and this gave Kaldor an idea of the
extensiveness of black money.

His calculations accounted for the depth of black
money circulating or lying in storage in the national
economy. The only difference might be, according to him,
the margin that would be entitled to tax relief and tax

24

exemption, if the black money could be converted into white money. He, therefore, had a fair enough conviction about the authenticity of his calculations.

In the course of his investigations, Kaldor had extensive discussions with businessmen, accountants, company directors, government executives, revenue officials and economists. The idea that he formed at this stage of the depth of tax evasion and black money ranged over a very wide margin, from 10 to 20 percent of the assessed income at the minimum to 200 to 300 percent at the maximum.

Then he went ahead with his computations, and assessed the possible scope of evasion and black money by determining the gap between national income estimates and public finance estimates.[2]

First approximation

The total of assessable incomes in all sectors outside agriculture came out at almost exactly twice the assessed income. Kaldor himself admitted that this estimate was not very precise, but then even in mining and factory industry, where specific statistics were available and where income was not subject to an exemption limit, the ratio was also 2:1.[3]

In his treatise, based on these conclusions, Kaldor went on to say that "if his estimations were anywhere near the truth", the amount of public taxation lost to the exchequer was of the order of Rs.200 to 300 crores (taxation on additional income correctly assumed is at least 40 percent).

This was a far cry from the estimate of only Rs.20 to 30 crores as sometimes quoted in this connection, and which at that time was more or less the official estimation voiced by the Board of Revenue of the Indian Central Government.[4]

In subsequent discussions, prior to an official investigation on the subject in 1970-71, Kaldor's estimates have been regarded as fairly authentic, as also scientific, as a first approximation.

The Direct Taxes Administration Enquiry Committee (1958-59), appointed by the Indian federal government however concluded that Kaldor's estimates were on the high side. They were prepared to admit that there might be another fifty crores in the storage as black money, but it could not be anywhere near Kaldor's estimation. The Committee however had extremely inadequate data to support its conclusions and depended more on feelers and impressions than pragmatic analysis.

One has to remember that this huge amount of black money does not however keep lying in the shade, but bulk of it is in circulation in clandestine deals, and that it spins money backward and forward. Right back in 1957, with a base of Rs.300 crores of black money, as

calculated by Kaldor, it could safely be estimated that
while one-third would be in storage, at least two-third
would be in circulation.[5]

In other words, pursuant to Kaldor's calculations,
we could compute a circulation of approximately Rs.400
crores of black money in the country, in 1957-58, compri-
sing of approximately Rs.100 crores spun back from the
money in circulation and those earning interest in
foreign banks, resting in shadow accounts or in other
forms of what may be called secondary liquidity.

Surprisingly, in addition to certain desultory
discussions, there has been no serious attempt (except
very lately) either by the government or by the economists in India to assess or contain the circulation of
black money, while over the years the forces of black
money were not only proliferating and helping to thrive
on expanding black market in the country, but were also
making inroads into international trade-channels through
smuggling and international speculation.

Committee of experts

The Ministry of Finance, Government of India,
appointed,by a resolution in March 1970, a Committee of
Experts to examine and suggest legal and administrative
measures for countering evasion and avoidance of taxes.
Justice K.N. Wanchoo, retired Chief Justice of the
Supreme Court of India, was the Chairman of the Committee
and this then came to be known popularly as the Wanchoo
Committee.

The Direct Taxes Enquiry Committee (DTEC) produced
their final report in December 1971. This Committee had
continued Kaldor's tentative research, based on many
assumptions and variables (due to lack of adequate
research having not earlier been done on the subject),
and gave a more or less authoritative estimate of the
extent of black money in the Indian economy.

Wanchoo Committee, for the first time, also gave a
precise definition of black money. It is, as its name
suggests, tainted money - money which is not clean or
which has a stigma attached to it. It symbolises money
which has been earned by violating the provisions of law
and even social conscience, and which is kept secret and
unaccounted for.[6]

In the economic literature of the 'forties,
references were frequently made to black market, as also
to black money operating such a market. Boulding here
and there in course of his writings on marginal analysis,
developed certain supply and demand models in a black
market, but did not try to correlate it to black money.

But it was during the Second World War that the
terms black market and black money really came into vogue,
and featured in discourses as inter-related phenomena.
In India, there has been only tentative discussions on

the subject by a few economic researchers like Hannan
Ezekiel,[7] S.K. Ray,[8] P.D. Gupta and C.N. Vakil.[9] But
even these discourses were more or less confined to the
operative aspect of the black market rather than on the
depth and extensiveness of black money. It is only
lately that the present author has written a number of
articles on the parallel economy, pertaining to its
emergence and proliferation in the Indian situation.[10]

Anyway, in their writings and also in official and
non-official references, the term black money became
current to describe the money received or paid in such
black market deals. Since disclosure of these deals,
which were entered into by violation of rules and regulations, would have invited severe penalties, these were
naturally not entered in the regular books of accounts
and, consequently, remained concealed from the ambit of
public finance. Thus a huge infrastructure of black
money rested in the national economy extending its sphere
of influence in black market and international trade, and
thwarting growth, planning, price stabilisation, public
revenues and investible surplus.

A wider concept

With the passage of time, black money acquired a
wider connotation, wider than its association with the
black market transactions alone. Today, the term black
money is generally used to denote unaccounted money or
secret income and/or undisclosed wealth as well as money
involved in transactions wholly or partly suppressed.

Some consider only that as black money which had its
origin in secret transactions made on the sly and is
currently in circulation.

There are others who consider this a narrow view of
black money. To them, black money denotes not only
unaccounted currency which is either hoarded or is in
circulation outside the disclosed trading channels, but
also its investment in gold, jewellery and precious
stones made secretly, and even investments in lands and
buildings and business assets over and above the amounts
shown in the books of accounts.

Today, when black money has come up to exert
definite and extensive pressures on the economy in India
and many other countries, the concept of black money has
been reckoned with as in the second interpretation
throughout the present treatise.

White money factor

In the deliberations of the DTEC, an intricate
interlinking has been established between tax evasion
and black money. While tax evasion leads to the creation
of black money, the black money utilised secretively in
business for earning more income inevitably leads to tax
evasion. While tax-evaded income represents black money
in a broad sense, all black money does not necessarily

originate in tax evasion.

Black money is also made through surreptitious use
of white money. In this sense, the proliferation of
black money derives an additional impetus from the intermixing of black income and white income. On the contrary,
some black money may be brought out in lawful investments
and expose itself to taxation.

This phenomenon was earlier mentioned while apprais-
ing Kaldor's estimates. There is always a measure of
money derived as black income which may be and are
converted into white income and thereupon come within
the taxation network. To this extent adjustments become
necessary in the computation of black money. Such
adjustments however do not become possible beyond giving
an allowance to what we may call white-money factor of
black money.

This is also true the other way round, in the sense
that to some extent accounted white money can be converted into black money. But this certainly requires
ingenuity and is replete with possibilities of detection.

A parallel economy

DTEC for the first time has emphasised the dual
nature of the national economy in India. Thus there is
an official economy, functioning on the basis of the
official monetary system, involving open transactions
financed through identifiable sources of funds, generating ascertainable income and wealth, and operating
generally in conformity with government rules and regulations and the levy system.

On the other hand, a parallel economy also functions
in India. This economy functions by waging open and
secretive competition with the official economy, a
simultaneous phenomenon at war at every stage with
government's monetary, banking and fiscal policy like
the tentacles of an octopus of the deep sea. As the
DTEC has pointed out, a secretive, defiant and an
unscrupulous element in our society provides the parallel
economy with its blood for sustenance.

It is based on the official monetary system, but on
a secret understanding and involves a complex range of
undisclosed deals and transactions pushed through
secretly with unaccounted sources of funds, generating,
in the process, income and wealth which escape enumeration or cannot be easily ascertained.[11]

While the present study is based on the Indian
economic situation, the demarcation of the national
economy between the official and parallel economies is
more or less universal in all free-market economies of
today's world, the difference being mostly of degrees.

Before we proceed with our studies on how black
money proliferates and how the parallel economy functions,
let us conclude our observations on the likely estimate

of black money in the national economy of India today.
Calculating further from Kaldor's computations, it was
estimated that around 1958-59 about Rs.400 crores of
black money were available in the economy, two-third of
which were in circulation, both in the national and
international money markets (concerning Indian exchange
accounts directly or even indirectly).

The Wanchoo Committee's estimates of income on which
tax was evaded are Rs.700 crores for 1961-62, Rs.1,000
crores for 1965-66 and Rs.1,400 crores for 1968-69 in
which year and loss of income tax revenue was estimated
at Rs.470 crores and the money value of transactions at
not less than Rs.7,000 crores.[12] (Cf. annexure 2).

Taking a mean of these figures, and allowing for
the white money factor, and the accepted rate of proliferation, the estimate of black money today in India is
expected to range between Rs.2,000 to 3,000 crores,
in absolute terms, and not in terms of money value of
the transactions they cover, which will be substantially
much higher.

The recent voluntary disclosures, operated by the
Central Government of India, have thrown up evaded taxation exceeding Rs.1,500 crores, and therefore it is
being voiced in many quarters that the extent of black
money in absolute terms may be well beyond Rs.5,000 to
Rs.7,000 crores, and in terms of money value of transactions covered, even beyond Rs.20,000 crores. These
however continue to remain in the nature of theoretical
calculations and not confirmed by documented estimates.

The estimate that approximately two-third of this
is always in circulation, and leading to further
proliferation, and one-third is in shade, continues to
be equally correct today.

The importance and implication of these figures
are profound and staggering. The tentacles of black
money have affected every sector of economic activity
in the country and thwarted the national effort to build
up the economy and despite increases in productivity
chained the economy with a galloping price spiral and
artificial and created and recreated shortages.

The Wanchoo Committee has elaborated this in a
precise manner... In the worst days of inflation, the
artificial element of shortages has always been large;
but as black money multiplied, the area of artificial
shortages seems to have grown. Even otherwise, the
distortions in the industrial economy, the periodic
foreign exchange crisis and the rigorous import curbs
have all provided a fertile field to anti-social elements
to ensure that their parallel economy is kept flourishing.
... Worse still, these illegal operations have induced
a considerable amount of leakage of foreign exchange
through under-invoicing and over-invoicing of foreign

trade deals, and also through secret cuts and commissions on joint ventures and collaboration agreements involving Indian and foreign parties. Small wonder then that there is, in this black money, a regular list of quotations covering items even where transferability is denied or restricted. These include industrial licenses, import licenses, allocations of materials, foreign exchange permits, etc.[13]

The parallel economy has unimaginably intricate ramifications. It thrives under the patronage of the unscrupulous element of our society which grows more and more defiant. It is based not on the official monetary system, but on a secret understanding and involves a complex range of undisclosed deals and transactions pushed through secretly with unaccounted sources of funds, generating in the process income and wealth which escapes enumeration and cannot be easily ascertained.[14]

Now we may analyse the effects of black money and its repercussions on the economy, in order to determine how the <u>parallel</u> economy distorts the functioning of the <u>official</u> economy.

The effect of black money on the economy of the country is nothing short of disastrous. It affects the public revenues, degenerates the investible surplus, delimits the national productivity, drains the balance of payments, distorts equity and equality concepts of economic distribution and halts and stagnates the planned programme for economic progress.

<u>Multiple repercussions</u>

The springboard for the rise and growth of black money is unaccountable and clandestine trade and commercial deals inside the country or across the border. The first casualty of black money therefore is revenue lost to the exchequer.

The major factor today that inhibits the optimum growth of the Indian national economy is the acute shortage of adequate resources needed for development, largely because a substantial proportion of the national resources lies enmeshed in black money in the parallel economy. As a result, such distress-concepts as the 'core plan' and even 'plan holiday' are often seriously considered. Black money goes hand-in-hand with tax evasion. Its forces, therefore, act contrary to the equity concept of taxation. Together, they throw a greater burden on the honest taxpayer and lead to economic inequality and concentration of wealth in the hands of the unscrupulous few in the country than anything else.[15]

Black money, shorn of its taxation liabilities, is cheaper than white money; it therefore naturally finds outlets in what is called conspicuous consumption through grandiose and ostensible expenditure. The

30

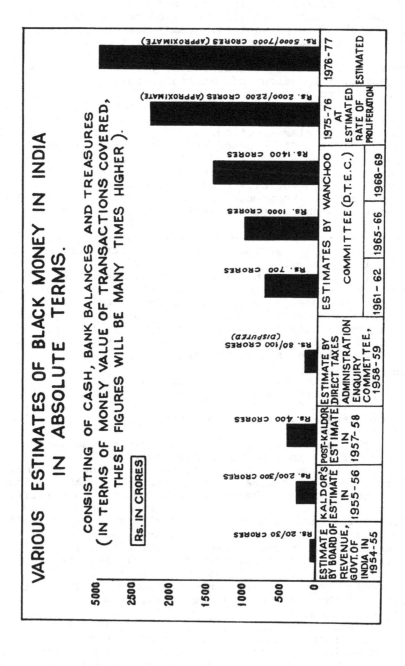

VARIOUS ESTIMATES OF BLACK MONEY IN INDIA IN ABSOLUTE TERMS.

CONSISTING OF CASH, BANK BALANCES AND TREASURES (IN TERMS OF MONEY VALUE OF TRANSACTIONS COVERED, THESE FIGURES WILL BE MANY TIMES HIGHER).

existence and proliferation of black money, therefore,
automatically leads to inflationary pressures, shortages,
rise in prices and economically unhealthy speculation in
commodities.

Earlier, we have explained the concept of black
money in shade; this, after conversion, takes the shape of
bullions, precious stones, jewellery and other valuable
articles, and again goes into shade. All these are
unaccounted but nevertheless potent money. The tendency,
and resultant strategies to acquire and conserve potent
money, leads to widespread smuggling in gold and silver,
precious stones and jewellery, national and foreign
currency across the national borders into the country,
draining our already strained balance-of-payments
accounts.[16]

Possessors of black money do not stop their manoeuvres even at this stage. They see to it that they
deprive the country of its wealth by transferring as
much as they can of their black resources to foreign
banks and trusts and deposits or clandestine investments
with their own associates. These are kept in shadow
accounts and accounts kept under the number system.[17]

A side-effect of this phenomenon is the oddity that
a country (India), where capital and more particularly
foreign exchange resources are scarce, becomes a defacto
lender of aid capital to economically advanced and
wealthier nations, with the concealed outflow of funds.[18]

It has been unofficially estimated that hoarded
black money, or black money converted in specie or
bullion or stones or jewellery, should represent almost
two-third of the country's investible funds thus
immobilised. They also tend to the production of non-
essential goods, where chances of detention are less and
thereby chase a substantial portion of the investible
surplus away from essential channels of investment.

The credit and investment policies of the government
are partially checkmated by the proliferation of the
black money in many channels. The government adopts a
policy of credit squeeze, while the black money sources
develop multiple leaks in its sources of funds. The
policy of credit squeeze would have no sobering effect
on investment channels. Similar facilities opened in
the parallel economy completely negative a dear money
policy that the government might have adopted.

Black money and tax evasion are even otherwise
encouraging over-financing of business which is as
dangerous as under-financing. These trends add further
to the inflationary pressures in the country. They can
undo also some of the major investment targets and
objectives of government's planning. Apart from the fact
that this situation results in an under-estimation of
resources in the country, thereby inhibiting investment

32

planning, there is reason to believe that the operation
of the black money economy has already upset the momentum
of economic development and distorted the pattern of
saving and investment in India.[19]
   One of the worst consequences of black money is its
pernicious effect on the general moral fibre of the
society. It has been said that black money places
integrity at a discount and puts a premium on ostanta-
tious display of ill-gotten wealth.
   Black money therefore is a cancerous growth, for
India as also for a number of other countries. If its
proliferation is not checkmated, it will further inhibit
national economic endeavours. The ways and means to
combat the forces of the parallel economy have been
developed in chapters 5 and 10.

NOTES

   1. Nicholas Kaldor - Indian Tax Reforms, Chapter 9.
   2. The results of his computations have been
summarised in chapter 10 of Kaldor's treatise in a table.
   3. Kaldor - Ibid.
   4. Speeches of the Union Minister for Finance
during the parliamentary debate on 1956-57 budget.
   5. S.K. Ray - Emergence And Proliferation of Black
Money; Economic Times, Bombay, May 3 & 4, 1978.
   6. Final Report of the Direct Taxes Enquiry
Committee, 1971, Chapter 2.
   7. Hannan Ezekiel - Black Money; Illustrated Weekly
of India, Bombay, October 17, 1971.
   8. S.K. Ray - Black Market; Indian Finance, Calcutta,
September 5, 1955.
   S.K. Ray - Economics of Black Market; Eastern
Economist, June 21, 1968.
   S.K. Ray - Black Market; Further Considerations;
Economic Times, October 21, 1973.
   9. P.D. Gupta - Black Money, White Money; Yojana;
March 14, 1965.
   C.N. Vakil - Measures to Check the Growth of
Unrecorded Gain; Supplement to Capital, December 24, 1964.
   10. S.K. Ray - The Parallel Economy; Business
Standard, Calcutta; January 6, 8 & 9, 1979.
   S.K. Ray - Emergence & Proliferation of Black
Money; Economic Times, Bombay, May 3 & 4, 1978.
   11. Final Report of DTEC.
   12. Final Report of DTEC, Chapter 2 (cf. annexure 2).
   13. Final Report of DTEC.
   14. Final Report of DTEC.
   15. Final Report of DTEC.
   16. Chapter 5, The Labyrinth of Smuggling.
   17. Ibid.
   18. Final Report of DTEC, 1971.
   19. Final Report of DTEC.

4

Many Faces of
the Black Market

A black market has more or less a vertical structure. It consists of several stages - successive, allied and, more often than not, interlinked. In each stage or tier again, there are several horizontal sectors, with the same pattern of complementary interrelationship.[1]

A pyramid

At each of these sectors, there are different types of manipulators, all working with a common objective, profiteering, and operating through the media of price-jumping or stock-racketing. In the different inter-mediate tiers and horizontal sectors, do function such operators or technicians of the black market as illegitimate speculators and price pullers, who directly or indirectly participate in the different sectors.[2]

Before we go into an investigation of the different sectors, it will be wise to undertake a cataloguing of these sectors as can be surfaced for the purpose of the present thesis. While doing so, our study may as well reckon with two aspects of such an analysis of the black market, viz., the organisational and the financial structures of the black market, which are different only in respect of their functional attributes, but are otherwise coextensive and inter-dependent.

The organisational structure of the black market can be discussed as under:

1. Cornering. Hoarding. Silos, cold storages and dark godowns. Retail and wholesale black market in commodities, particularly elastics and near-elastics, consumables and building materials.
2. Black market in production. Spurious commodities. Adulteration. Fakes and imitations. Jumping of standards. False packaging and labelling. Rackets in supply. Rackets in exports and imports. Substitution.
3. Economics of black market in scarcity. Sharking on crop and production failures. Black market during famines.

33

4. Illegitimate speculation. Gambling. Stock
market rackets. Foreign-exchange rackets.
Permits, licenses and fake trade deals. Ghost
transactions in lands, hundies, shares, properties and investments.
5. Tax evasion.
6. Smuggling and international trade rackets.

Cornering and hoarding

Cornering is the first step towards the creation of
a black-market build-up. As we have discussed earlier,
a fluctuating price level is normally the best working
media for a black market operative. A fluctuating price
level may be attained by spreading false reports as to
the state of supply or, more frequently, of demand; or
more probably by buying and/or selling in direct opposition to such reports to twist the price-spiral upward or
downward.[3]

This points to certain basic black market strategies,
cornering being the objective which they finally intend
to achieve. By different devious means effort is made
to make the prices of a commodity to fall, or even crash,
and then to buy up the commodity in huge quantities and
corner the same.

As a black-market strategy, cornering is the first
step towards hoarding. Hoarding takes place when the
suppliers purchase out the entire, or bulk of a commodity,
and block the same, without there being any fall in
demand or, what is commoner, in the face of increasing
demand. This sag in supply in relation to demand results
in serious upturn of the price spiral.

What happens at this stage has been almost a daily
experience during the last decade not only in the Indian
markets, but also in the national markets of many other
countries. At this point, the commodity is smuggled to
the black market where it is unsealed little by little
and an artificially inflated profit-ratio is secured.

Cornering and hoarding, between them, take control
of the supply situation of the black market, and thereafter go to manipulate the forces of demand, so that by
the forces of interaction, black market profit could be
maximised.[4]

Apart from the case of vegetable oil, as developed
earlier in chapter 2, there have been similar instances
of cornering and hoarding of steel, cement and other
building materials, with similar interaction on economic
forces of supply, demand and prices for these commodities.
In country-wide raids, huge quantities of hoarded steel
pipes and ingots were unearthed in India and much more
disclaimed and many big names featured in the raids
conducted by the government during 1974 and 1975 mainly
in Delhi and Calcutta metropolitan areas.

Where are these commodities hoarded ?... In view

of frequent raids conducted by several agencies under the
government and the civil administration, the operators in
the black market are careful about the venues of hoarding.
Silos and cold storages are normally used for such hoarding; but since these are the cynosure of all eyes, whenever such hoarding is arranged in silos and godowns, or
in houses and flats, mansions and bungalows, elaborate
frauds are committed in respect of the accounts books,
so as to cover up both the transactions and the hoarding,
and for this purpose sometimes even the books of accounts
and stores ledgers and inventory charts are all
duplicated.[5]

Dark godowns

Normally, however, such surreptitious hoarding is
arranged in a number of off-beat godowns, not only in
towns and cities, but also in the countryside.   This is
done by the owners of warehouses and godowns, and
sometimes even flats, mansions and dak bungalows are
purchased or taken on hire by such persons for black
market hoarding of commodities.

In the massive dehoarding drive on cereals in 1975,
it was reported in the press that even school buildings,
panchayat offices and temples were used for such hoarding. To beat all, is the news carried in the Statesman,
Calcutta on September 13, 1975:

"Bhopal, Sept.12 - Some hoarders in rural areas
are keeping their goods in monuments, reports UNI.
Civil Supplies officials in Sagar district claim
to have seized 60 quintals of wheat hidden inside
a tomb near Shahgarh village in Banda tehsil."

Earlier, there were reports in the press which
indicated considerable risk and ingenuity deployed by
black market operators in hoarding, when a mosque in
Bihar was defiled by hoarded cans of kerosene oil, and
steel tubes were hoarded in a pond covered by hyacinth
near Calcutta in the heyday of the drive against the
black market in steel trade.

Hoarding becomes malignant to the society when
necessaries, and other inelastics, such as wheat, sugar
or textiles, are hoarded. These, and a range of
agricultural and quasi-agricultural commodities, have
inelastic demand attributes. Irrespective of their
supply situation and prices, and irrespective of the
income levels of the consumers, the demand curve flows
steady for such commodities.

These commodities are, therefore, ideal for the
black market operators. These commodities, being highly
responsive to the black market strategies, are the first
and the commonest prey to the black market and the
largest share of cornering and hoarding, therefore,
takes place in respect of these commodities.

Even though not agricultural or quasi-agricultural,

certain other commodities like hard and soft coke, iron
and steel, cement and building materials, and drugs and
pharmaceutical commodities, are also highly susceptible
to cornering and hoarding; these commodities, being in
the nature of <u>necessaries</u> are governed by economic
forces of demand and supply similar in character to those
that influence inelastic commodities.

Commodities, especially agricultural commodities
and necessaries, have rather inelastic demands (and
frequently supplies, if the market was free), and, therefore, changes in underlying conditions governing either
(as is done in the black market) of these commodities
cause quite disproportionate rises in prices, and
consequently in income distribution.[6]

There is consequently much political pressure for a
policy of stabilising agricultural prices by government
action. The so-called valorization schemes in cereals,
rubber and coffee, 'the ever-normal granary' and the
crop-restriction schemes of the New Deal, were all
attempts made in the U.S.A. at such stabilisation.[7]

Same compulsions of economic distress of the common
people are responsible for the wrath and popular condemnation that widespread cornering and hoarding of essential
agricultural commodities and necessaries, all with
inelastic demand attributes, evoked in India. The same
compulsions again account for the drives and government
action against cornering and towards dehoarding.

Black market in a number of countries like India
has permeated even the stages of production, even before
the produce has been slated for distribution. The different manifestations[8] of black market in production may
consist of one or the other or a group of the following:
> adulteration;
> imitations and fakes;
> jumping of standards;
> false packaging and labelling;
> production of spurious commodities; and
> substitution and rackets in supply.

Adulteration
Adulteration, beginning from the second world war,
has today become, what may be called, <u>big business</u>. The
ways and methods of adulteration, as have come to light,
are myriad. The menace had become so pestering in India
that the government was obliged to set up a Committee to
go, inter alia, into such devices of adulteration and to
devise ways and means for their eradication.

This Committee as also institutions like the Indian
Toxicological Research Centre have made independent
investigations on such rackets. As a result of these
researches, there have been startling revelations about
how menacing are the extent and proportions of adulteration in India today.[9]

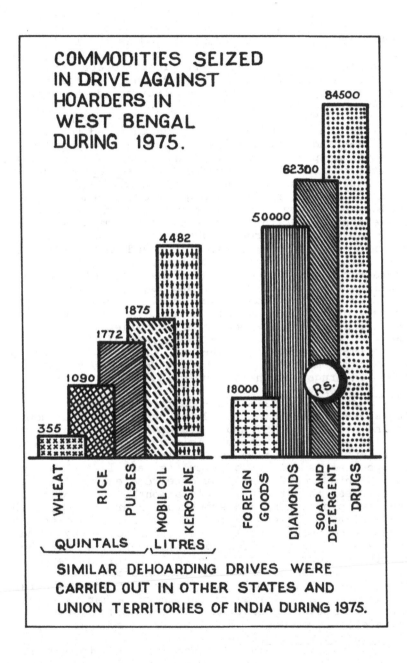

COMMODITIES SEIZED
IN DRIVE AGAINST
HOARDERS IN
WEST BENGAL
DURING 1975.

84500

62300

50000

4482

1875

1772

1090

355

18000

WHEAT

RICE

PULSES

MOBIL OIL

KEROSENE

FOREIGN GOODS

DIAMONDS

SOAP AND DETERGENT

DRUGS

QUINTALS LITRES

Rs.

SIMILAR DEHOARDING DRIVES WERE
CARRIED OUT IN OTHER STATES AND
UNION TERRITORIES OF INDIA DURING 1975.

Adulterators have adopted modern technology in a big way for their mixing business. While the traditional method of adding harmful foreign bodies to staples continues, sophisticated mixers have transferred certain latest technology from factory floors to adulteration sheds. In some cases, the production line itself is modified to produce inferior quality or adulterated goods.

It has been revealed recently that a number of spurious industries had been using advanced techniques. Capsuling and strip-packing machines are prepared to be employed in pushing out pills and capsules resembling reputed brands. This is called misbranding in law.[10]

Adulteration today has become a multi-pronged menace. This started in a big way during the second world war, by the sharks in the black market. The trend has expanded over the years and has become diversified, and from milk and cereals, adulteration has spread to cooking oils and medicines, spices and pharmaceuticals.

Akin to adulteration, other trades similar in character but all undertaken in the quest of black market profiteering, are imitations and fakes, jumping of standard, false packaging and labelling and large-scale production of spurious commodities. A large number of these instances have been lately revealed by the researches conducted by the scientists of the Indian Toxicological Research Centre and several sub-panels of the Hathi Committee set up by the Union Government of India on drugs and pharmaceuticals.

Anti-adulteration law

There are certain anti-adulteration acts,[11] legislated by the states and the centre, and put down in the statute books, and infrequent and sporadic arrests and law-suits under the provisions of these acts have been reported from time to time in the Indian press. But enforcement is full of difficulties and lacunae and the punishments provided are not deterrent enough.[12]

Unless the criminal implications of adulteration, spurious productions and substitution are recognised by the society and highly deterrent legislation is enacted, lip-service pseudo-legal measures are not going to be of much avail. If the recent drive, undertaken in rather desultory spurts in recent years in India, had any temporary dampening effect on adulteration and such other devices, it should be attributed to the temporary fear of the law-enforcement machinery rather than to any deterrent statutory enactments. The need for the latter, therefore, is evident, in India, as elsewhere.

Black market in scarcity

The height of black market atrocities is committed during conditions of scarcity and crop failures, and is at their acme during famines. The basic economic forces are, however, two; first, unchanged or sometimes increasing demand chasing a contracted and gradually tottering supply, worsened by cornering, hoarding and downright black marketing; and secondly, strategies adopted in the black market for naked profiteering.

Price control and rationing, in a market influenced by black market operators, complicate matters further. What happens, when price ceilings are imposed and rationing introduced, without other restraining deterrents ?... The immediate result is a shortage.

If a commodity becomes scarcer in an unregulated market, the result is a rise in its price to the point where purchasers accommodate themselves to the smaller amounts forthcoming. The commodity does not altogether disappear from the market; stocks are always available for purchase by those who are fortunate enough to be able to afford the high price in the black market. If, however, the law prevents the price from rising to this equilibrium-level as the black market profiteers would want it to be, stocks disappear from the market as buyers snap them up faster than they are being replaced.

The rate of purchase is forced down to the rate at which the commodity is reaching the market, not by the restrictive operations of high prices but by direct restrictions of one sort or another on the ability to purchase.[13] The degrees of cornering and hoarding would actually determine the range of black market prices.

These economic forces, and their interplay, can be manoeuvred to heighten the margin of profiteering in the black market if there is a precipitate crop failure and failure in food-import arrangements, either or both resulting in acute shortages. Hoarding in such circumstances becomes most malignant to the society.

In course of the scandalous Bengal famine of 1942, during the second world war and before the Indian independence, there was black marketing in paddy, rice, wheat and all other foodgrains, black marketing in its worst manifestations, cornering and hoarding, brazen black market sales at highly inflated prices, beyond the reach of all ordinary levels of purchasing power. While thus the black market racketeer amassed huge tainted profit and acquired real estates and black market treasures, people suffered untold misery and even died in thousands.

Unlawful speculation

Black market speculative rackets lead to violent fluctuations in prices and lead to block-transfer of white money into black channels and group-involvement of black money into unlawful speculative rackets.

Contrary to popular belief, unlawful speculation is perpetrated not only on the floors of stock exchanges, but in many sectors of the black market and in rackets

involving controls, licenses and permits, all of which
usually involve misfeasance of the worst variety.
In the market of unlawful speculation, gambling and
clandestine rackets, there are multiple ways in which
black money earned in black market spins to generate
more black money at the cost of the people. One marvels
at the ingenuity of the unlawful speculator and the
devices adopted by him.
It is found widely used for conducting speculative
business transactions in what may be called Account No.2,
cornering of shares and debentures, smuggling of gold,
diamonds and luxury articles, unauthorised transactions
involving foreign currency and purchase of scarce
commodities for the purpose of hoarding, further speculation, increased profiteering and black marketing on the
rebound.
Such black money keeps on spinning around further
speculative deals and transactions. It is spent in
purchasing by unlawful means quotas and licenses at
premia, in call deposits, bogus loans, ghost hypotheca-
tions, acquisition of movable and immovable assets
(e.g. jewellery, tax-free government securities),
deposits in Indian and foreign banks in ghost or
numbered accounts and real estates purchased in real and
fictitious names, often with on-money speculative
payments.
In spite of the vigilance exercised by the government, controls and regulations frequently come to be
used by the unlawful speculators and other unscrupulous
elements in the society for infiltrating white money into
black channels.
Since considerable discretionary powers lay in the
hands of those who administer controls, these often
provide them with scope for under-hand deals — speed
money for issuing licenses and permits, and hush money
for overlooking jumping of controls and rationing.
All these, ever since the second world war, have
given rise to speculative trading in permits, quotas
and licenses, malpractices in distribution and, in the
process,   generated sizeable sums of black money in
India. As the transactions in violation of statutory
restrictions and speculative deals and trading in
permits and licenses had to be entered into surrepti-
tiously, these had necessarily to be kept back from the
tax-authorities and these, therefore, led to tax
evasion.[14]

Smuggling

This has been dealt with extensively later in this
thesis.[15] Black market, black money and smuggling are
inextricably interwoven and are only but stages of
development of a similar process of behind-the-screen
but extremely potent economy.

As we have discussed later, smuggling in today's
world has since covered a few more ugly milestones, and
is now done not only in gold and specie, precious commodities and antiques, but also in uranium and state documents, and sometimes, even verge on international
espionage.[16]

Tax evasion

Another face of black market and black money is tax
evasion. As the black market proliferates, black money
is spun; but this remains overwhelmingly outside the
network of public finance, except for expenses incurred
by black market profiteers and other owners of ill-gotten
black money in conspicuous and ostentatious living.

Research work on tax evasion in India is limited.
Attempts to estimate and study tax evasion suffer from
some basic infirmities owing to the insufficiency or
non-availability of reliable data. Unless a detailed
breakdown of the total assessed income generated in each
year is available, it is difficult to make a scientific
study of tax-evasion.

Some data for 1961-62 could be obtained from the
Directorate of Inspection (Research, Statistics and
Publication). An exercise on the basis of the data was
made by the Direct Taxes Enquiry Committee. The conclusion of this study is that the income which escaped tax
for 1961-62 would be of the order of Rs.811 crores.

The estimates of tax evasion in India made by the
Direct Taxes Enquiry Committee can be summarised from
the Committee's Final Report as under:

1. Applying the ratio of evaded income to the
   assessable non-salary income of 1961-62 to the
   assessable non-salary income of 1965-66, the
   evaded income for 1965-66 works out to
   Rs.1,216 crores.
2. Even after making adjustments on inadequacy of
   information and such other limitations, the
   estimated income on which tax has been evaded
   would probably be Rs.700 crores and Rs.1,000
   crores for the year 1961-62 and 1965-66 respectively.
3. Projecting this estimate further to 1968-69, on
   the basis of increase in national income, the
   income on which tax was evaded for 1968-69 can
   be estimated at a figure of Rs.1,400 crores.
4. The extent of income tax evaded during 1968-69
   would be of the order of Rs.470 crores, being
   one-third of Rs.1,400 crores. The money value
   of deals involving black money may, therefore,
   be not less than Rs.7,000 crores for 1968-69.
5. The tax-evaded income is not all lying hoarded
   which can be seized by the authorities; much
   of it has been either converted into assets or

spent away in consumption or else is in circulation in undisclosed business dealings.

Taking a mean of these figures, we had calculated
earlier in this thesis that, allowing for the white money
factor and the accepted rate of proliferation, the
estimate of income evaded today would be rather staggering and, reckoned in money value of deals, assets and
transactions covered, this would be nothing short of
fantastic.[17]

It may be kept in view that all tax-evaded income
is not generated in the black market, but bulk of it is.
At the same time, most of the tax-evaded income, for the
purposes of public finance, constitutes black money,
which may rest idle in the shadow, or be converted in
gold, silver, real estates and treasure, or as is the
case with most of the tax-evaded income, be ploughed into
black market and multiple black money channels.

DTEC has indicated the basic reasons[18] of tax
evasion as under:
1. Deterioration in moral standards.
2. Corrupt business practices.
3. Ineffective enforcement of tax laws.
4. Economy of shortages and consequent controls
   and licenses.
5. Donations to political parties and purchase of
   political cover and protection.
6. High rates of sales tax and the levies.
7. High rates of direct taxation.
8. Ceiling or/and disallowance of business
   expenses.

While detailed measures to unearth black money and
fight tax evasion will be investigated in depth in the
last chapter,[19] we may enumerate here some of the basic
steps considered by the DTEC:

Measures for unearthing black money
1. Voluntary disclosure scheme.
2. Revamping the settlement machinery.
3. Issue of bearer bonds.
4. Authorising opening of Swiss-type bank accounts.
5. Authorising canalisation of black money into
   social, philanthropic and other specified fields.
6. Vigorous searches and seizures.

Measures to fight tax evasion
1. Reduction in tax rates.
2. Simplification of taxation.
3. Minimisation of controls and licenses.
4. Regulation of donation to political parties.
5. Creating confidence among small taxpayers.
6. Allowance of certain business expenses.
7. Wide changes in penal provisions.
8. Vigorous prosecution policy.
9. Wider taxation of agriculture income.

10. Streamlined intelligence and investigation.
11. Compulsory maintenance of accounts.
12. Substitution of sales tax by excise duty.
13. Compulsory audit of accounts.
14. Wider power of survey.
15. Wider punitive surveillance on ownership flats,
    pugree payments, valuation of real estates, tax
    evasion in entertainment industries, share
    transfers and foreign exchange violations.

Financial structure of the black market

The most important source of money supply for the
black market is black money. Black money is found
widely used for conducting concealed business transactions, to finance and refinance cornering and hoarding,
purchasing illegal quotas and licenses at premia (for
further resale in the black market), financing secret
commissions, financing ghost hundi and share transactions. Black money is also the source for financing
international black market deals and smuggling of
commodities both-ways for their further black-marketing.

Then there is drainage of white money into black
market. This has been discussed in chapter 3 as white
money factor. While tax-evaded income represents black
money in the broad sense, all black money does not
necessarily originate in tax evasion. Black money is
also made through surreptitious use of white money. In
this sense, the proliferation of black money derives
an additional impetus from the intermixing of black
income and white income. On the contrary, some black
money may be brought out into lawful involvements and
do expose itself to taxation.

There is always a measure of money derived as black
income which may be and are converted into white income
and thereupon come within the taxation network. To this
extent, adjustments become necessary in the computation
of black money. Such adjustments, however, do not become
possible beyond giving an allowance to what we may call
white-money factor of black money.

The other aspects of black market financing consist
of bilateral or multiple financing in shady international
deals, acquisition of assets in the black market for
financing and refinancing black market transactions,
financing through shadow accounts and parallel banking
system and high-money financing for smuggling and
international black market.[20]

Group sense

One basic texture in the firmament of the black
market is a group sense and moral code amongst high-shark
black marketeers. It is only the retailer in the black
market who may occasionally indulge in rate-cutting.
Normally, however, both in the retail and the wholesale
black market, there is a group sense of comradery, and

44

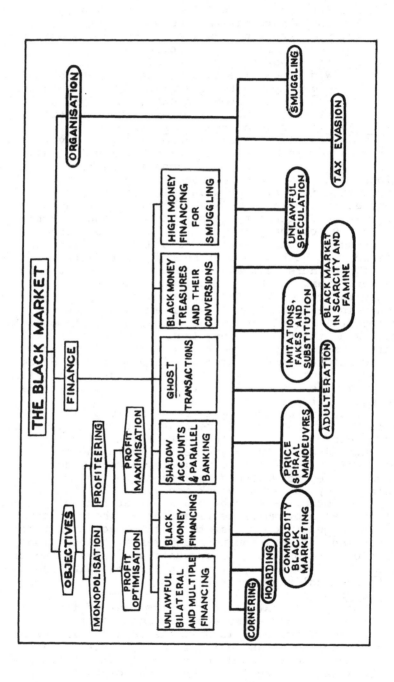

the operators work more or less in concert, in order to
boost the prices upward or downward, in consonance with
the demand and supply characteristics of the commodity
cornered and hoarded and the percentage thereof intended
to be released in the black market, so that the maximum
turnout of profit is realised by the brotherhood of the
black market.

To this end, there are publicists, rumour-mongers
and an intelligence system in the black market. There
are what may be called inter-sectoral intelligence,
mutual alliance and coordination in the black market.

Like many faces of the eternal Eve, the black market
also has multiple faces. While in this chapter we have
unravelled the different faces, the remedial strategies
for combating each would be analysed in subsequent
chapters. Myriad are the ways and the sectors of the
black market; the strategy therefore also has to be
many-splendoured.

NOTES

1. S.K. Ray - Theory of the Black Market; Eastern
Economist; New Delhi, June 21, 1963.
2. S.K. Ray - The Profiteering Curve; Financial
Express, Bombay, May 9, 1977.
3. Clay - Economics for the General Reader.
S.K. Ray - Cornering, Hoarding And Price
Behaviour; Financial Express, Bombay, March 10, 1978.
4. S.K. Ray - The Profiteering Curve; Financial
Express, Bombay, May 9, 1977.
5. S.K. Ray - Company Fraud, Liability of Auditor
and Jurisprudence; Economic Times; January 26, 1974.
6. Boulding - Economic Analysis (1955); Hamish
Hamilton, London.
7. Boulding - Ibid.
8. S.K. Ray - Many Faces of the Black Market;
Business Standard, Calcutta, June 1 & 2, 1978.
9. Report of the Indian Toxicological Research
Centre; Hindustan Times, New Delhi, September 11, 1975.
10. Prevention of Food Adulteration Act, 1954,
amended upto 1975.
11. Prevention of Food Adulteration Act, 1954, (Act
XXXVII of 1954), amended upto 1975, is the principal
fountain of such law in India.
12. Sections 16 to 21, ibid.
13. A fuller discussion of the effects of price
control and rationing on a market vitiated by the forces
of the black market has been undertaken in Chapter 10,
Strategy For A Combat.
14. Direct Taxes Enquiry Committee, India, Final
Report.
15. Chapter 5, The Labyrinth of Smuggling.

46

16. Chapter 5, <u>The Labyrinth of Smuggling</u>.
17. Chapter 3, <u>The Parallel Economy</u>.
18. S.K. Ray - <u>Many faces of the Black Market</u>;
Business Standard, Calcutta, June 1 & 2, 1978.
19. Chapter 10, <u>Strategy for A Combat</u>.
20. S.K. Ray - <u>Emergence and Proliferation of Black
Money</u>; Economic Times, Bombay, May 3 & 4, 1978.

5

The Labyrinth of Smuggling

During the last few years, a floodlight of attention has been focussed in India, as in many other countries, on what are being called economic offences. It is not correct that the expression has been coined in the wake of the recent drive in India against smuggling. The concept has been in vogue in the theory of public finance since long.

Economic offences

In India, however, economic offences as a concept gained currency through discourses of Nicholas Kaldor on Indian public finance.[1] Economic offences, however, are not confined only to surreptitious deals in international trade. These may consist of tax evasion, black marketing, speculation in currency, illegal share transactions, unlawful ghost investments and such other acts of omission or commission.

In the present chapter, however, we are concerned with that part of economic offences which has a direct or indirect bearing on a country's international balance of payments, and are perpetuated through jumping or cornering the law on trade between India and any other country. The principal aspects of such economic offences rest in the multi-faceted activities lumped together as smuggling.

Related to smuggling, and arising out of it, are such offences as international speculation in bullion, specie, gold, jewellery etc., or in the shape of opening and operating of shadow or numbered accounts in foreign banks, or in arranging and perpetuating trade channels with a view to evade the statutory and conventional laws on public finance of the home or foreign country, and all the while generally working contrary to the national development programmes. All these are known as smuggling of one sort or another.

An evil influence

Smuggling has become an evil influence in a number of economic systems like the Indian. Smugglers today

47

represent a very important element of the money market, credit structure, stock exchange and financial system generally. In the wealth and treasure they have accumulated behind the screen of public finance, they do effectively control, with other subterranean forces, what may be called a parallel economy, with intricate efficiency.

Together with the black market operators, they represent the black-money economy of the country, which according to the Indian Direct Taxes Enquiry Committee, 1971, is an extremely potent evil force. Over the years, the parallel economy has grown in size and dimensions... In this parallel economy, there is apparently no shortage of anything, no lack of facilities, and certainly no lack of money, provided the price is suitably <u>black</u>.[2]

An ordinance, and later an enactment, to combat smuggling was promulgated in 1974 by the Indian Central Government, popularly called COFEPOSA.[3] These had armed the government with substantial authority to take action against smugglers. The ordinance and subsequent enactment, and a chain of arrests of top-notch smugglers under the latest provisions of law, put the floodlight on smugglers and smuggling in India throughout the second half of 1974, 1975 and early 1976. Earlier to this, and as a sequel to the arrests, there was extensive debate in the Indian Parliament on the subject.

In course of the debate, perhaps for the first time, the government had indicated that smugglers have assumed substantial financial power. A Union Minister of State for Finance advised the Parliament that smuggling had lately assumed great dimensions and that smugglers had amassed huge wealth and attained social status.[4]

Buying their way through, with bribes and favours, the smugglers did acquire strength to challenge the very fibre of economic and political system. They could maintain their own wireless systems, speed-boats, convoys of trucks, jeeps and motorcars with fictitious number plates and a local army of aides and helpers all over the country. They had spread their tentacles over business houses, industries, share markets, motion pictures, construction industries and other walks of life with impunity. They had built multi-storeyed buildings and palaces for themselves, using their resources derived from smuggling.[5] This is true of many countries.

Extent of smuggling

What is the extent of smuggling in India ? What is the extent of money and wealth that smugglers control in the Indian econo-financial structure ?

These two questions are very difficult to answer. For one thing, the whole affair is behind-the-screen and surreptitious. Secondly, one has to depend for such estimation mainly on the seizures and accountals by

Income Tax and Customs authorities, and the area they can cover by the very nature of things can be a part of the spectrum. Thirdly, the estimates by economists and politicians are ridden with assumptions and are frequently in the nature of guestimates.

Dr. V.K.R.V. Rao[6] gave an estimate of the extent of smuggling current in India now during the aforesaid parliamentary debate. Dr. Rao's estimate had a ring of authenticity in view of the fact that his assessment was, it is believed, worked on certain pragmatic researches, based on information available from certain official and non-official sources.

Dr. Rao told the Indian Parliament that goods worth Rs.300 to 400 crores were being smuggled into the country and that this was an important source of black money. There is, however, every reason to believe that the amount may be, and in fact is, far in excess of this figure due to tremendous increase in smuggling ever since 1970. In the first five months of 1974 alone, 35 Arab dhows were caught on the Arabian sea-coast of India, whereas in 1970 the number was only three.[7]

Let us now turn to official sources of information. According to W.C. Wagh,[8] smuggling in India today is "foreign trade without government sanction and running of a parallel banking system." He estimated the turnover of the parallel central banking system alone at Rs.2,000 crores.[9]

Objectives

Smuggling may be done in many ways, and it may involve many commodities from prosaic items of merchandise like pulses and barn to consumables of sophistication like vintage wine and priceless jewellery, and from gold biscuits to antique images. More of its modus operandi will be discussed later. The objectives behind smuggling however are mainly three:

1. Conversion of foreign exchange abroad by unlawful means and plough-back of such illegal exchange-currency to finance smuggling into India;
2. Despatch by sea, air or land, gold, specie, jewellery or other contraband into India in surreptitious ways;
3. Conversion of the rupee obtained through the sale of contraband into foreign currency or other commodities like silver, antiques, rose-wood etc. to be smuggled out of India, or for investment in hotels and motels, cinemas and theatres, bars and kiosks, red houses and call-girl bureaus, sky-scrappers and factories, or in affluent living outdoing the Indian Maharajas.

It is easy to appreciate that the whole range of objectives for smuggling is against the rule and letter of law all the way. As the Wanchoo Committee of India stated, the smugglers have no shortage of money, provided the price is sufficiently black. A principal dictum in the smugglers' underworld is that there is nothing that money cannot buy. The situation as regards the smuggling network is identical in a number of other countries surveyed for the present treatise.

Black money, in any shape and quantity, therefore, is used by the smugglers to grease and blaze their way through, in order to achieve any one or more of their objectives. In the process, blood may spill, witnesses may disappear, evidence blotted out, and honesty made a scapegoat. In a complete absence of morality, anything goes for a smuggler, across the frontiers of any single country.

Smuggling: modes and forms

Smugglers usually collect their booty of precious foreign exchange abroad in one or more of the following methods:

1. Gross underinvoicing of exports;
2. By smuggling silver out of India;
3. Overinvoicing of imports against licences for goods for a small margin of profits;
4. Purchase of foreign exchange from Indian residents abroad by making compensatory payments to their relatives and friends in India;
5. Smuggling out narcotics;
6. Transferring of curios and antiques to countries where they fetch fabulous prices;
7. Purchasing foreign exchange from tourists; and
8. Export by ghost firms and subsequent non-realisation of the proceeds in India.[10]

These different modes of smuggling can be further explained as under:

1. Underinvoicing means invoicing of goods at a price less than the price for which they are actually sold to the foreign buyer. The local exporter and the foreign buyer reach an understanding about the price to be actually paid and the price to be indicated on the relevant documents. The difference between the two is made up and deposited in foreign banks and in shadow accounts.
2. The annual smuggling of silver is estimated to be substantial. It is sold at a lower price abroad as payment for goods smuggled into the country, like gold, synthetic yarn, watches, etc. According to rough unofficial estimates, silver hoards in India amount to about Rs.1,000 crores.
3. The overinvoicing of import against licences for goods is done by foreign parties on the basis of letters of credit provided to them by their local counterparts. The difference is used to support

illegal transactions.

4. The latest trend in foreign exchange rackets deals with securing hard currency from residents of a country abroad by making compensatory payments to their relatives and freinds in the country. It is estimated that 70 percent of smuggling is financed by foreign exchange generated by deflection of inward remittances into unauthorised channels.

5. Until the passage of the recent bill by the Indian Parliament, no law regulated the sale of antiques in India. It is learnt that Indian antiques fetch fantastic prices in affluent Europe and U.S.A. No government agency so far has been able to estimate the amount of damage done to India's ancient heritage and perhaps it might never be possible to evaluate the colossal financial loss.

6. The supply of unauthorised foreign exchange through purchasing currency from tourists in the country is also substantial. The transaction is mostly through taxi drivers, hoteliers and tourist guides.

7. Ghost firms invariably export goods and disappear without leaving any trace. The Reserve Bank of India allots a code number to every member of the Export Promotion Council; in the case of ghost exporters, the procedure is breached.[11]

Gold racket

It is no major secret that the proportion of privately hoarded gold is substantial in countries like India. Gold used to be hoarded by the rich, the maharajas, nawabs and chieftains through the ages, and the trend got a spurt during the British regime. With the emergence of smuggling in virulent form in today's world during the last two decades, there has been a spurt in the hoarding of gold.

The seizures of gold by the Preventive Collectorate, Bombay, during the years 1971, 1972 and 1973 amounted to Rs.8.58 crores, 11.53 crores and 14.22 crores respectively. But these seizures, according to the authorities, are less than 10 percent of such gold.[12] It is commonly believed that about this much seizure is provided for a normal trade fluctuation by the racket, and that only about twenty-five percent seizure may really tell upon gold smuggling and bring it down sizeably. About fifty percent seizure may render the racket unprofitable.

Gold reserves with individuals and trusts in the country add up to a few thousand crores, according to an unofficial estimate.[13] One shudders to think of the staggering amount, particularly when one remembers that this idle resource would very easily see India through

52

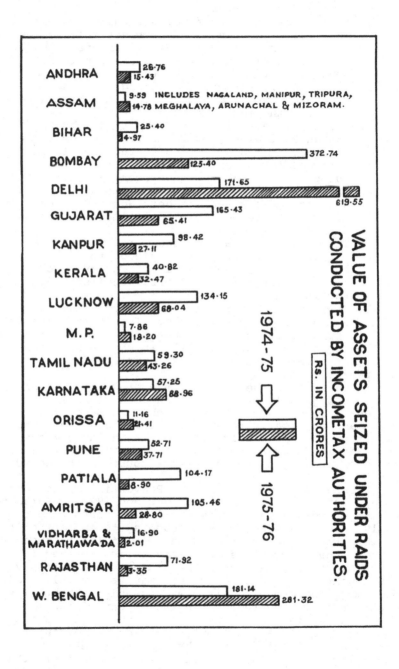

VALUE OF ASSETS SEIZED UNDER RAIDS CONDUCTED BY INCOMETAX AUTHORITIES.

Rs. IN CRORES

1974-75

1975-76

State/City	1974-75	1975-76
ANDHRA	26·76	15·43
ASSAM	9·59	14·78
BIHAR	25·40	4·97
BOMBAY	372·74	125·40
DELHI	171·65	619·55
GUJARAT	165·43	65·41
KANPUR	98·42	27·11
KERALA	40·82	32·47
LUCKNOW	134·15	68·04
M. P.	7·86	18·20
TAMIL NADU	59·30	43·26
KARNATAKA	57·25	88·96
ORISSA	11·16	24·41
PUNE	52·71	37·71
PATIALA	104·17	8·90
AMRITSAR	105·46	28·80
VIDHARBA & MARATHAWADA	16·90	2·01
RAJASTHAN	71·92	3·35
W. BENGAL	181·14	281·32

ASSAM INCLUDES NAGALAND, MANIPUR, TRIPURA, MEGHALAYA, ARUNACHAL & MIZORAM.

her present financial stringency and shortages in invest-
ment-potential for a few five year plans, without the
need for debt-servicing and deficit budgeting.[14]

Recent exposures

Smuggling is financed by black money, both in settlement of exports and imports in the underworld. During
the winter session of the Indian Parliament in 1974-75
there were many startling exposures on the floor of the
Lok Sabha and the Rajya Sabha by members of both the
party in power and those in the opposition.

Certain reputed newspapers and periodicals of India
also had deployed their established reporters and
correspondents not only to cover the debates, statements
and discourses in and out of the Parliament, but also to
follow their own leads, make important scoops and do
researches on their own.

Some of the recent exposures have brought about
specific information about smuggling being financed and
generally covered by black money. Some of these are
chronicled in the subsequent paragraphs.

Transactions worth Rs.7,000 crores, financed
entirely by black money, were carried out in two years
(1974, 1975), according to the income-tax authorities.[15]
Most of this money often changed hands in ghost transactions in immovable property deals.

It was not that this entire amount came from black
money resources, for the smugglers had their own means
of transferring some of their resources into white money
as also innumerable links with the official economy. On
the other hand, it cannot be said for sure that this
estimate covered the extent of smuggling in its entirety.

It has been reliably estimated that over 60 percent of lands, buildings and flats in urban and metropolitan areas in India are sold with documents showing
fictitious prices, grossly undervalued. In many of these
deals, 40 to 60 percent of the money is often paid in
black. Through undervaluations, parties are able to
evade income tax, wealth tax, capital gains tax, gift
tax, estate duty and stamp duty. The real income on such
black money transactions consequent upon income derived
by smuggling is more than easily realised, as is the
aggregate loss to the exchequer. Besides real estate,
black money is also invested in bullion, jewellery and
commodities in short supply.[16]

According to the Income Tax Department, a distressing trend among professional people like lawyers, doctors
and architects is to refuse payment in cheques for
their services. This is indicative of how a trend is
being fostered even by professionals to pile up black
money. It is also learnt that a number of such professionals are sustained at fancy prices by the smuggling
underworld with black money.

The most startling channel of smuggling that has raised its ugly head is in uranium, a rare radioactive mineral, highly priced for its use in nuclear devices. Smuggling in uranium is not only absolutely anti-national, but also involves evil hair-raising escapades by the underworld operators. Their manoeuvres remind one of the escapades by diamond smugglers against which the fictional hero James Bond marshalled his genius.[17] Deaths, murders and tortures of innocent people, including nuclear scientists, have been reported in connection with such smuggling.[18]

The trend indicates the following disturbing features in smuggling in the world:

1. The craft of smuggling is no more confined only to the usual channels, but has crossed into dangerous and highly anti-national avenues.
2. Smuggling has become highly well-organised, brutal and a cult where anything goes.
3. Smuggling has generated areas of influence and protection and are frequently fostered and protected by the same.
4. There may be a growing shadow of foreign agents in smuggling in a number of countries and it will not be incorrect to think that there may be espionage links.

Inter-state leakages

An offshoot of smuggling is what may be called inter-state leakages of grains. This is a phenomenon which started during the British days in full glory around 1942, when the notorious Bengal famine took a horrible toll of human lives.

This is a natural corollary to prohibition on inter-state movement of foodgrains except through authorised channels. Gangs and speculators became active after independence, when prohibitory orders were imposed by the government on free movement of foodgrains on public account from surplus states.

The intention of the government was to arrange an equitable distribution of foodgrains between surplus and deficit states through such agencies as Food Corporation of India.

Inter-state leakages in grains immediately started, by the grain racketeers, through surreptitious channels, which bought their way through, from surplus states to deficit states and also to adjoining countries.

This is a common experience in many countries of the world today, countries that are afflicted with scarcity of foodgrains. In respect of a number of countries in South-east Asia, New Africa and Latin America, the phenomenon has ultimately hit the man in the street very badly.

Bootlegging

There was a fortuitous circumstance in India which made the underworld blossom into hundred different ways. This is the introduction of prohibition in the country partially in 1937, and in many states after independence. Illicit distilleries sprang up overnight and had extended the tentacles and crossed the national frontiers principally to the Arabian Sea coast. Many lawyers also flourished, defending cases against bootleggers.

A class of social workers also arose; they provided sureties for the distillers or helped them through the police prosecution and saw to it that illicit breweries were not raided.

As a matter of fact, to begin with, the members of the legal profession who defended cases against smuggling, black money, tax evasion, adulteration and similar offences made substantial money, and became the first important props for the underworld.

It is futile to say that smuggling across the borders has been in existence even in the Muslim period. That it was, but it was nothing more than a clandestine trade channel, and except for loss of revenues, it had no other socio-economic implication. Even the loss of revenues was only marginal, as taxation (and public finance) was not intricate.

The umbrella

Smuggling, particularly in its present structure, is a British legacy in the Indian sub-continent. Both the parallel banking system and their clandestine network have been handed over to our smuggling underworld by the foreign regime before Indian independence. There are, however, no records or documents available about this transfer of power. According to researches made on the subject, smuggling in those days had obvious links with the espionage system and the secret service. The foreign rulers opened banking houses for the smuggling network at a number of towns abroad through which huge sums were transferred to all for payment to general intelligence. It is said that this banking system later provided the nucleus for the parallel banking system of the underworld in the Bombay area.[19]

It is, however, said that the British had set aside two secret landing facilities for foreign or Indian smugglers to land at Bandra Chimboy and Utten near Bombay.[20] After the racketeers took over the war-time network, they acquired more landing places. Slowly and silently they started infiltrating their channels of influence.[21]

The underworld is reported to be replete with distinguished names of lawyers, social workers and contact-men, many of whom in later life carved out their links in politics. This provided a soothing umbrella for

those in smuggling and international money-racketing,
within and across India and a number of other countries,
the coastal towns and villages on the Arabian Seaboard
in particular providing the launching pads.[22]
    In the late 'fifties and the early 'sixties, a new
class of people had come to dominate the world of
smugglers. Young, reckless and daring young men of
dubious social background, but ambitious all the same.
They provided just the material the bosses were looking
for. Even when such men were caught and jailed there
was nothing to lose by way of social honour or family
repute. It is said that most of the men who have finally
emerged as leaders of smuggling gangs were orphans or
social drop-outs.[23]

Brief offensive

    The offensive started in 1974 in India against
smuggling. There were multiple arrests in many parts of
the country. In the network of arrests were caught many
sharks which were top-notch operatives in the smuggling
underworld and international racketeering concerning the
Indian sub-continent. There was an immediate effect on
prices which first showed a downward trend and then
indicated a tendency to stabilise at a comparatively
lower level. (Please see annexure 3).

    This drive, which has been covered extensively
later in this chapter, however, suffered a serious
setback when some top smugglers, who were detained under
the latest Act were set free by the court, due to
certain apparent loose ends in the prosecution cases and
also in the law on the subject.

    Encouraged by this, there were a plethora of liti-
gation launched by the smugglers and their aides. There
were a few cases also under the Habeas Corpus Act. The
smugglers have no dearth of money and they have been
able to deploy the best available talents for legal
defence.

    The government, it appeared, was caught up in a
string of time-consuming litigations, which were proving
costly to the exchequer. The government also discovered
certain gaps in the enforcement and prevention laws. The
Indian judiciary has the highest prestige for its
impartiality, but has to be guided by the law of the
land.

    The government, therefore, was obliged to pause and
ponder, as to the next steps required to be taken, which
of necessity were to be within the precincts of the law.
The releases of detenus by the court, and a few veiled
strictures in the judgments, brought about immediate
jubilation in the underworld. This was evident from
certain statements made by the kings of the underworld.

    It was no secret that the smuggling rings which
were in a large measure thwarted by the government, again

collected their reins, and resumed their activities.
Their leadership, which was whisked away by the government by a large number of detentions, being thus partially restored,there was evident resumption in their
activities.

A brief idea may here be given of the direction of
the offensive by the Centre and some of the States in
India from around 1974. Among the raids the one conducted by the Customs officers at Bombay was dramatic. The
Customs authorities used the speed-boat Vasavi to
capture a brand-new craft valued at Rs.5 lakhs and
recovered synthetic fabrics valued at Rs.10 lakhs.
Immediately after the seized craft was taken out at
midnight when signals flashed by a vessel were noticed
and two boats were found to be moving towards each other.
The customs authorities made a dash and intercepted a
smugglers' craft coming from Dubai. When the customs
officers put the ropes on the intercepted craft they were
cut by the smugglers who then attempted to escape. A
fresh chase was given by the customs authorities and both
the smugglers' craft and the other boat which was going
to meet it were captured. This dhow yielded 22 packages
containing textiles, chemicals, metallic yarn and
calculating machines valued at Rs.11.5 lakhs. The value
of the Arab dhow is about Rs.1 lakh.

A drive had also been maintained on sale and open
display of smuggled goods on the pavements and in the
fashionable markets in the metropolitan cities. A
special watch had been kept on different channels of
sources of supply of smuggled goods. On July 2 and 3,
1975, in two days, thirty-five raids were carried out
on shops and stalls, in the four metropolitan cities of
Bombay, Madras, Delhi and Calcutta and goods worth
Rs.16.25 lakhs were seized. Six persons were arrested.
On July 3, 1975, the Bombay Customs authorities raided
the Navajeevan Cooperative Society, Chembur and recovered
contraband textiles valued at Rs.28,000 from a common
passage of a building.

A truck coming from Bombay towards central India
was intercepted at Kota and four packages containing
2,477 wrist watches of foreign origin valued at Rs.4
lakhs were seized. At Bombay two trucks were apprehended
with 94 packages of contraband textiles at Reti Bander.
The value of the goods seized was approximately Rs.13.66
lakhs.

It was reported from Ahmedabad, date-line July 27,
1975, that a big vessel, costing about Rs.400,000 belong-
ing to an alleged smuggler of Surat was attached by the
Gujarat income-tax authorities at Dahanu port in
Maharashtra. The authorities also found out a ghost flat
worth Rs.1.5 lakhs held by the same smuggler in Bombay.

According to an official press release, this was a

sequel to searches carried out by the Gujarat income-tax authorities at Surat, Daman, Bombay, Jaipur and other places in the cases of persons alleged to be involved in smuggling activities.

The authorities also discovered another flat in a posh locality of Bombay - which allegedly belonged to a top smuggler of Daman. Both the smugglers were taken in custody and their properties seized.

Arrests of smugglers had humbled the bullion market, at least temporarily. It was reported in the press that the news of the arrest of top smugglers caused a sharp setback in bullion prices at Bombay on July 2, 1975. Spot silver declined to Rs.1181 from the previous closing of Rs.1207 a kg. At one stage during the day, it was quoted as low as Rs.1176 a kg. Similarly, standard gold fell to Rs.542 from Rs.549 for ten grams.

The above instances reflected that the government machinery was being mobilised against smuggling. Unfortunately, it had stuck aground in the midstream in 1976.

The law

It has been said that there is no advantage in preaching the gospel to a bunch of crooks.[24] Similarly, there is no point in advising restraint and counselling patriotism to smugglers. They only understand the red eyes of the law.

No other agency but the government can, therefore, put down smuggling effectively. For this, enforcement agencies must be fully equipped with the necessary legal cover. Only prerequisite is that the government in power should not only take to it as a temporary expedient, but as a manifesto given to the people and adopted as a firm policy of economic strategy, under appropriate parliamentary cover of both economics and jurisprudence.

The drive against smuggling, started for some time in 1974 in India, unveiled in the subsequent months certain gaps in the law, which were taken advantage of by the smugglers in courts. Arrested ringleaders were released and certain steps taken by the government (without adequate preparatory measures as required under the law having been taken), were also frowned upon in certain law cases.

For a long time, the laws of the land in India were rather ill-equipped for such a fight. The Sea Customs Act was inadequate as a measure for preventing smuggling. Under it the onus of proving that the seized goods were smuggled lay on the Customs Department, whereas in the case of gold, silver and wrist-watches (covered by Section 123 of the Customs Act), the onus lay on the passenger to prove that he was innocent. It had been suggested that textiles should also be included in the list of notified goods under Section 11 of the Indian Customs Act.

It has to be appreciated that jurisprudence is no

freshman's job. Therefore, instead of trying to cover
the gaps in the law against smugglers and smuggling,
through a number of hastily drafted ordinances, coming
one tumbling over another, the juristic position may be
expeditiously studied by acknowledged economic and legal
experts, and adequate enactments passed by the
parliament. (Please see annexure 3).

Enforcement of these laws would then have to be
pursued vigorously and the smuggling rings effectively
liquidated. Smuggling is a vice, which is like a hydra-
headed monster and cutting a few heads would not be
adequate. All the heads should be chopped off and the
smuggling rings annihilated completely.

Finally, it is to be hoped that under a proper
legal enactment suitable steps would also be taken in
relation to the parallel banking system, its assets
taken over and added to the national exchequer, along
with shadow accounts in other banks.

The next step to be taken would be, in liaison with
foreign governments, to proclaim and take over as
national funds, the shadow accounts built up by smugglers
in foreign banks. The legal and diplomatic implications
in this regard need to be examined urgently.

An idea recently being advocated is that ringleaders from the smuggling underworld may be given a
political amnesty on their renouncement of ill-gotten
wealth and assurance of turning a new leaf. This can be
of very limited value, for sooner it is appreciated that
the real fight is against smuggling as such, rather than
some individual smugglers, the better. Winning over or
even liquidating a few top-notch smugglers is only
but a step towards the achievement of the total objective,
which is annihilation of the smuggling underworld, and
the government's policy has to orient itself to the said
objective.

Remedial strategy

To sum up, in order to liquidate smuggling the
following measures will be required to be taken:
1. Enforcement of law. Intensive raids aiming at
   prevention of tax evasion, unearthing of black
   money from lockers, shadow accounts and other
   sources and on haunts of smuggling need to be
   made extensively. Raids on sea, air and land
   routes also need to be intensified.
2. Detention of smugglers. The known smugglers
   should be rounded up and detained, so that they
   cannot proliferate their trade. They have
   certain important links, which include racketeers,
   espionage agents and others; these persons
   should also be detained.
3. Action under the process of law. Suits should
   be submitted at courts of law against persons

held under 1 and 2 above and their conviction sought by the government.

4. <u>Strengthening the hands of enforcement agencies.</u> This is of extreme importance, not only to provide them legal cover, but also protection as necessary. Their job involves risk and should have adequate financial incentive. The strength of such agencies should also be increased as multiple and frequent raids would be required.

5. <u>Plugging loose ends of law.</u> Comprehensive and adequate enactments need to be made to cover the loose ends of the different statute laws. As a matter of fact, it would be wise to compile and pass a comprehensive act relating to smuggling and smugglers by land, sea and air. The subject should be probed in the first instance by acknowledged experts in jurisprudence and the law knit up clause by clause, before the same is presented to the parliament for enactment.

6. <u>Seizure of properties.</u> Properties in the shape of cash, jewellery, bullion, landed property, buildings, hotels, bars etc. of smugglers convicted or gone underground to escape the hands of the laws should be seized and accredited to the government. Legislation to this effect should be formulated. This should preferably be incorporated in the comprehensive statute suggested in 5 above.

7. <u>Nationalisation of smugglers' banks and seizure of shadow accounts.</u> The real strength of the smuggling rings lies in their parallel banking system. An ordinance and enactment for their <u>nationalisation</u> and seizure would also appear necessary to strike the final nails on the coffin of smuggling.

It is disappointing that a string of steps as outlined above have never really been taken, not only in India, but in many a country beset with the smuggling network. It is to be hoped that the trend would finally be taken to its logical conclusion and would not as usual end up in only a matter of the moment. Smuggling to the economy is just as malignant as cancer to a human body. Deliberate, well-conceived and precipitate strategies are required to be taken by the government to achieve the objective of a lasting annihilation of smuggling and liquidation of all its bastions.

NOTES

1. Nicholas Kaldor from Cambridge University visited

India in 1955 and investigated on tax evasion. His treatise, <u>Indian Tax Reforms</u>, was published next year from London.

2. Final Report of Direct Taxes Enquiry Committee, India, 1971.

3. <u>The Conservation of Foreign Exchange and Prevention of Smuggling Activities Act</u>, 1974; No.52 of 1974.

4. Stated by Mr K.R. Ganesh, Union Minister of State for Finance, during a debate in the Parliament in the winter session, 1974.

5. Ayub Syed - <u>Smugglers in the Net, What Now</u> ?;The Illustrated Weekly of India; Bombay, November 1974.

6. Dr. Rao, a noted Indian economist and one-time Vice Chancellor of the Delhi University, was an ex-Union Minister for Finance, and, later, Transport.

7. The Indian Express; New Delhi, September 29,1974.

8. W.C. Wagh was in overall charge of anti-smuggling operations under the Government of India during 1974-75.

9. Reported in the Illustrated Weekly of India, Bombay, November 10, 1974.

10. Ayub Syed - <u>Smugglers in the Net - What now</u> ?; The Illustrated Weekly of India, Bombay, November 10,1974.

11. Ibid.

12. Ibid.

13. Reported by a Special Correspondent in the Times of India group of papers during September 1974.

14. Ibid.

15. Revealed to the press by the Income Tax Department, Government of India.

16. S.K. Ray - <u>Smuggling Network</u>; Economic Times, Bombay, June 24 & 25, 1978.

17. Ian Fleming - <u>Diamonds Are Forever.</u>

18. <u>Smuggling of Uranium</u> - A Special Correspondent; Illustrated Weekly of India; Bombay, November 10, 1974.

19. Ayub Syed - <u>Smugglers in the Net - What now</u> ?; ibid.

20. Ibid.

21. Ibid.

22. Ibid.

23. Aruna Mukherjee - Indian Express, Bombay, a series of articles in September 1974.

24. C. Bresciani - Turreni -- <u>Economic Policy for the Thinking Man</u>; William Hedge & Co. Ltd., London, 1950.

6

Price Behaviour
Since Independence

An immediate indicator of the forces of the black market at play is the range of fluctuation of the price spiral. It will, therefore, be relevant if an analysis is made of the behaviour of the price level in different sectors of the Indian economy since independence, both in respect of wholesale and sectional prices. It will be also in the fitness of things, if, while making such an analysis, an attempt is also made to delink the factors responsible for price hikes at different periods of time. While doing so, an endeavour will also be made to locate the forces of the black market and black money at play.

A graph of the price spiral drawn during the first four five-year plans in India depicts the face of a sea hit by a hurricane with very occasional lulls in the wind. During the periods of the lulls also, the price level rested not at the bottom of a valley, but rather on the height of a plateau.

Structural imbalance

When organised state planning was taken in hand in India, the background was as laden with arrears of development as in case of Soviet Russia before the advent of the Gosplan. There were huge leeways of structural imbalance of the economic firmament[1] and great burdens of population rehabilitation. It was not possible for the economy to take off to a programme of intensive industrialisation, in view of the necessity to first remove sectoral and disguised unemployment and reduce unemployment in absolute terms.

A poor gross national product confronted the multitude with little or no purchasing power, while the prices were high. The wholesale price index was 4.5 times the pre-war index. Working class cost of living indices for different industrial sectors reached three to four times the pre-war level. Partition deprived India of considerable sectoral economic balance by taking away jute and most of the cotton and also part of silver,

63

gold and exchange reserves.

This was not all. Emergence of planning in India had also to wade through a 52 percent increase in population over the first half of the century, poor labour-absorption ratio in agriculture, a low productivity slate and resultant stagnation in both agronomy and industry, and finally, in the shape of the ultimate economic consequences, erosion in both per capita income and standard of living of the people.[2]

In short, the first five year plan, apart from handling the responsibility of rehabilitation, was also committed to the problems of a typical underdeveloped economy.[3]

The objectives of the first five year plan for their implementation, however, depended on large-scale borrowing from abroad and deficit budgeting. While this was so, trouble also arose with hybernating capital, available in the black market, and in the shape of black money, generated during the war and post-war years, when scruples were thrown to the winds.

This money was available with the nouveau riche, many of whom continued to practise the craft of the black market learnt during the war years. Again and again, during the first few five year plans, the efforts of the government for increasing productivity and containing the price spiral were vitiated by the forces let loose by the black market and the parallel economy.

The background

The present discussion has, therefore, to begin with a consideration of the questions pertinent to the behaviour of prices in economic development and the growth of the gross national product. In this context an overwhelmingly important and relevant question is whether inflation generates economic growth. Time and again deficit financing has been championed on the ground that an inflationary fever in prices helps to generate greater economic activity and larger national product.

This, unfortunately, is diametrically contrary to the work-a-day experience of the average Indian. The statistical evidence available for the Indian economy suggests that rising prices discourage economic development and rabid inflation, in fact, seriously inhibits growth.[4]

As a matter of fact, this has been no unique experience for the Indian economy alone. There is, for instance, the well-known Latin American example. Economic development in Latin America in an environment of rabid inflation actually suffered and the set-back caused to the economy by inflationary financing finally called for a reversal of the economic policy.

In the case of a number of Asian countries also,

forces of inflation are increasingly proving detrimental to growth. The experience even of the advanced countries points to the view that inflation renders the process of growth more difficult and that it has to be avoided for social and economic reasons.[5]

There is a whole panorama of discussion on inflation in economic literature, from Keynes to Einzig and from Einzig to Kurihara; this has spotlighted the adverse effects and limitations of inflation as a means to economic growth. From a study of such literature and the background of the Latin American and Indian experience, it can be emphatically stated that inflation is a socially costly and economically wasteful means of increasing investment.[6]

The reasons leading to this conclusion can be summarised[7] from available economic literature as under:

1. The redistribution-effects of inflation are extremely averse to equity in income distribution, and leads to arbitrary losses to low and fixed income groups and windfall profits to those advantageously situated; the black market operators and black money jugglers are prima donnae amongst the people so advantageously situated.

2. Inflation affects savings and investments adversely. While its ability to force savings is limited, inflation seriously throttles voluntary savings.

3. Inflation guides a flight of savings into non-productive channels through hoarding in specie, gold, metals and bullion, excessive inventories, acquisition of real estate, foreign balances, shadow accounts and money in lockers.

4. Inflation dampens economic motivation, as there is a general breakdown of economic morale, what with easy money with the new rich and a trend towards piling of money and treasure in the shade. This is to a large extent because inflation and black money move hand in hand.

5. Inflation exposes the government to budgetary miscalculations and generates problems of higher wage bill, oncost on administration and higher operating ratio of the public sector. All these do reduce available resources for development. or lead to further inflationary financing.

6. In all inflationary markets, exports became less profitable, partly because home demand is diverted to them, and partly because exports become too expensive to be worth the while. Depleting foreign exchange receipts on the other hand affect the country's capacity to import.[8]

7. Inflation detracts the attractiveness of foreign

investment essential for a developing country to
supplement resources. In case of a developing
economy suffering from a fundamental disequilibrium which is structural in character, inflation
flourishing under the manoeuvres of the parallel
economy gives rise to a number of distortions
in the economy.[9]

Plan objectives

Before getting down to an actual analysis of the
price behaviour, we may review the objectives and
pattern of the first four five-year plans. These are
very relevant to the consideration of price level, which
was governed not only by the forces of black market and
black money, but also the forces let off by the plan
strategies.

As for objectives of the first plan, it was felt
that the government adopted the concept of a mixed
economy with a dominant role for the public sector; the
accent was on industrialisation, specially the development of basic and capital goods industries, as from the
second plan period; also fiscal expansionism without
inflation and the maintenance of exchange stability; and
substantial dependence on external assistance with a
view to its early elimination... Not all these four
elements were clearly perceived or formulated right from
the start. The first plan was modest in almost every
way. The mixed economy concept was expanded largely in
terms of complementarity of the two sectors, although
stress on public savings and investment was unmistakable;
there was more stress on the infrastructure for development than on industrialisation as such; the role of
deficit financing was envisaged as just marginal, no
more than that of countering the deflationary effect of
the proposed draw-down of sterling balances; and, while
the plan showed an awareness of the emerging gap between
external receipts and payments, the question of foreign
aid or any strategy in respect of it was yet nowhere in
the picture.[10]

In other words, the first five year plan aimed at
nothing more than clearing the underbrush, for the
outlook on investment was bleak and there were uncertainties about the applicability of extensive deficit budgeting as a vehicle for economic planning. Emphasis on
industrialisation however came with the second, third
and fourth plans.

During this period there grew the theory of the
big plan with larger reliance on deficit financing and
countervailing controls... The bout of fiscal expansion
that commenced pretty soon after the launching of the
second plan reacted dramatically and menacingly on the
foreign exchange situation. A vigorous search for
foreign aid was thus started... Of the four crucial

ideas of India's development planning, the stress on
stability of the purchasing power (internal and external)
of money laid at the initial stages continued to recur.
The degree of emphasis laid on other ideas was, however,
different in successive plan periods.[11]
     These factors had their sway on the price level.
Investment grew, so did the growth of paper currency
with deficit financing and debt servicing with foreign
aids. Production increased but the prices also merrily
galloped away.
An undercurrent
     Here lay submerged in the whole process of economic
introspection a matter of great pity. There was, as has
been brought out in the earlier chapters of the present
study, no dearth of adequate economic resources to
finance a few successive plans, but this lay largely in
the shape of black money and in the labyrinth of the
black market and international smuggling, while the
country had to get submerged into an avalanche of public
and foreign debts to increase investment under the plans
for larger production and building the infrastructure for
greater industrialisation.[12]
     It was commented in this context that the task of
letting investible surpluses emerge first in private
hands and of directing them subsequently into public
investment was, it was felt, an unnecessarily difficult
and tortuous one. It was far better, the reasoning
proceeded, to make large investments in the public
sector, to secure surpluses through them and to plough
them back directly into further public investment... The
private sector would in this situation continue to expand,
the public sector would grow much faster, so that within
a measurable period, it would come to occupy the command-
ing heights of the economy and would be able to direct
and manoeuvre the rest of the economy into the desired
patterns of growth.[13]
     This idea received an impetus in the second plan
when the ratio of investment in the public and private
sectors went up to 55:45 from 46:54 in the first plan.
The third plan envisaged a ratio of 65:35, a slower rate
of change compared to the second.
     These, therefore, were the assumptions on invest-
ments and growth, and these assumptions held the field
in our plan strategy during the currency of both the
second and third plans. As for the fourth plan, the
basic concepts did not really alter.
     The assumptions of the planning strategy catapulted
the foreign and public debt investments, but did not
lead to proportionate rise in productivity, exchange
balance or standard of living, because of the set-off
value of inflation and price-hike which actually led to
a fall in standard of living, rise in production-cost,

and made exports less viable financially. The gnawing
forces of black market, smuggling and black money made
costing of expansion and growth to jump and did eat away
plenty of our investible surplus.

This was not all. The third plan registered a
shortfall in performance owing to many abnormal factors.
There were two border conflicts and two severe draughts
together with some unfulfilled assumptions, e.g. delay
in external credits and flight of surplus into black
money channels.

Over the third plan the rate of growth of national
income (in real terms) was less than half of the target
rate of five percent. Agricultural production did not
show any increase except in 1964-65. Industrial production was lower than expected. The ratio of savings to
national income which had risen from 5.5 percent in
1950-51 to 9.7 percent in 1960-61 was only 10.6 percent
in 1965-66.

The ratio of net investment to national income was
13.5 percent in 1960-61 and 13.1 percent in 1965-66. A
serious inflationary situation (had thus) developed,
exports received severe setback and the rupee had to be
devalued within a few months of the conclusion of the
plan.[14] In the process, Mr. Sachin Chowdhury came and
went as the Union Finance Minister of India.

The continuing stagnation

Sectoral imbalances continued even at the beginning
of the fourth plan. This reflected that all the
measures adopted for economic development had not
really bloomed up the economy towards stability and
prosperity for the multitude, and there was all along an
undercurrent of economic forces which exerted a
contradictory influence. In our opinion, black money
and the forces of national and international black market
might have played a major role amongst factors inhibiting
the matching growth of the economy and dragging of
development.

The principal instances of such maladjustments are
summarised below in brief:

1. Employment, even at levels of under-employment,
   was still in the rural sector of the economy,
   which accounted for fifty percent of the national
   income. Industrialisation as yet did not account
   for anything more than a superstructure.
2. The pattern of land ownership and tenancy
   arrangements, fluctuations in agricultural
   production and a galloping price level and
   relative underdevelopment of organised markets
   materially influenced the distribution of income.
3. The flight of industrial income to a concentrated
   coterie and to black money led to further distortions in the equity of income distribution.[15]

4. A considerable portion of output in the rural
   sector was retained by producers for self-consum-
   ption and a significant proportion of rural
   investment was direct. Much of the transferable
   savings came from the non-rural, non-agricultural
   sectors. These savings, strangely enough, were
   also stockpiled as hoarding of commodities and
   accumulated money and treasure in shade.
5. By far the largest majority of the population
   was unable to provide for itself adequate
   housing, education and health facilities. The
   basic infrastructure still remained insufficien-
   tly developed, while on the other hand, income-
   disparities and monetary-gimmicks in the black
   market exerted their own influences on the
   economy.[16]
6. The major part of exports consisted of products
   of agriculture, agriculture-based industries and
   mining, and imports largely consisted of capital
   goods and industrial manufactures. Thus even
   after a decade of organised state planning, the
   pattern of exports and imports did not materially
   change even though these were all part of a
   strategy to build up a favourable balance of
   payments.[17]
7. A low level of income accompanied by a low level
   of savings compelled the government to substantially erode its foreign balances for purposes
   of developments. This made the international
   exchange account of the country relatively
   weaker when it needed to be further propped up.
8. There was disparity in income distribution or
   consumption standards and concentration of
   economic power. The distortions became manifest
   with the prosperity of the black market and
   expenditure, at show-off levels, from the hidden
   vaults of black money.

But things were not really that bad, as development
of the economy, as a sum-total effect of the planning-
process was catching up, and there were silverlines,
of which the following were particularly relevant to
the growth of the economy:

1. Gradual assumption of a definite shape of the
   infrastructure of the economy typified by the
   emergence of a new entrepreneur-class along with
   the production of an increasing volume of
   producers' goods;
2. The export-push provided by devaluation to
   entrepreneurship;
3. A steady growth of institutions for financing
   various sectors of the economy under State
   auspices; and

4. The gradual development of the agricultural
   sector characterised by confident and wide use
   of improved techniques.[18]

Delinking inherent forces

In recent years, ever since the fourth five year
plan was taken on the anvil, and in course of the fifth
plan, some rethinking on the planning strategy has been
taking place. While this is so, the need for delinking
the forces of black market and black money, from those
of currency supply and inflation on the one hand and of
production and investment on the other, needs to be fully
appreciated. Simultaneously, a real econo-juristic drive
to counter their effects is also necessary.

At the same time, one also becomes aware of a few
other characteristics in economic policy which are rather
ambivalent. For example, if the price of foodgrains was
to be controlled, the cost involved would bring about a
shift in investment pattern. Also, the policy of
liberalised industrial licensing could not be reconciled
with the growing role of distribution of imported scarce
materials through public agencies in 1969.[19] But, to
some extent, these were not filaments of a long-term
strategy but corrective steps aimed at specific economic
ailments of the day and therefore should be reviewed as
such.

It was commented in the context of the fourth five
year plan that the upward pressure on prices and costs
must at no stage be allowed to go so far as to necessi-
tate far-reaching, semi-permanent price and distribution
controls; and secondly, as soon as any price control
was imposed, steps should be taken simultaneously to
increase supplies by suitable adjustment of production
incentives so as to prepare the way for its timely
elimination... The major criterion in this field also
had to be the reactions of these controls on the development impulse, the fostering of which, at a number of
points simultaneously, was crucial to development of the
Indian economy during the fourth plan.[20]

Prices and costs, however, kept on increasing,
bringing in its wake rationing and control and state
trading, the working costs of which also meant heavy
overheads, and, thereupon, more increase in prices.
The system of controls again was rather halting and
half-hearted, and these, therefore, did really have no
far-reaching influence on the market or any sobering
effect on prices. On the contrary, they enabled the
black market to play their aces well.

Against this brief general background, an analysis
can now be made of the behaviour of the price level in
India since independence, during the period of organised
state planning. While doing so, the nuances of the
price rise and their implications on the economy will

also be brought out.

General price level

The analysis of price trends given in this study is based on the wholesale commodity price indices published by the office of the Economic Adviser, Department of Currency and Finance, Reserve Bank of India, and as brought out in the monthly issues of the Reserve Bank of India Bulletin.

The limitations of these price indices data may, therefore, be emphasised before we proceed further. The official index which is currently in use has the year 1952-53 as the base for comparison, while the weight base of the index relates to 1948-49. Due to structural changes in the economy, brought about by plan-investments and certain maladjustments in the economy, production patterns and marketing trends have undergone changes, particularly in certain sectors. There is, therefore, the natural apprehension that the index based on 1948-49 weight may not always provide a proper measure of the impact on prices of supply and demand conditions at present.[21]

This, we have to admit, is an inherent constructional deficiency of the index. There are a few other limitations of a general nature, which have to be borne in mind for purposes of the present study. The index numbers of wholesale prices are designed to measure changes in the level of commodity prices at the non-retail stage of distribution and do not, therefore, provide a proper measure of the final prices charged to the consumer... Moreover, the all-commodity (whole-sale) price index is open to the criticism that it is a summary measure of all commodity price changes; but in summarising all changes the economic significance of them appears to be sometimes lost.[22]

A factor which again limits to some extent the significance of the indices for price analysis is price regulation, either statutory or informal, and another is distortion caused by black market manoeuvres to factors influencing the range of prices.

Wholesale prices

Trends in the wholesale prices have been summarised in Table 6.1 for the first three plan periods.

Before we proceed to analyse the trends of wholesale prices as depicted in Table 6.1, as to their portents and directions, it will be relevant to appreciate the compound rate of price rise for the general index and for major groups of commodities, on the one hand, and the index number of wholesale prices, on the other. (Tables 6.2 and 6.3).

A comparison with the index number of wholesale prices with 1952-53 as base will be relevant.

72

Table 6.1
Percentage variation in the wholesale prices

Group	Wei-ghts	First Plan	Sec-ond Plan	Third Plan	Second Plan Annual	Third Plan Average
All commodities	1000	-17.3	+35.0	+32.2	+6.3	+5.8
Food articles	504	-23.0	+38.6	+40.7	+6.9	+7.2
Foodgrains	235	-22.4	+39.9	+47.1	+6.9	+8.0
Tobacco & liquor	21	-17.8	+35.7	+24.3	+6.4	+4.8
Fuel, power, light and lubricants	30	+ 2.8	+26.1	+27.5	+4.8	+5.1
Industrial raw materials	155	-24.3	+46.9	+30.1	+8.4	+5.8
Manufactures	290	- 3.4	+24.3	+20.4	+4.5	+3.8
Intermediate products	41	-10.9	+30.5	+31.9	+5.7	+5.8
Finished products	249	- 2.2	+23.3	+28.4	+4.3	+3.5

Source:

Reports on Currency and Finance, 1967-68; R.B.I. Bulletin, June 1965 & June 1967; Economic Survey, 1961-66, Government of India.

Table 6.2
Compound rate of rise in prices (percentages)

Index	15 Yrs 1950-51 to 1965-66	10 Yrs 1955-56 to 1965-66	Third Plan Period 1960-61 to 1965-66	1961-62 to 1962-63	1963-64 to 1965-66
General index	2.7	5.9	5.8	1.2	8.9
Food articles	2.8	6.9	7.1	2.5	10.3
Industrial raw materials	2.5	6.7	5.4	-3.2	11.5
Manufactures	2.4	4.1	3.8	2.1	5.0

Source:

R.B.I. Bulletin, June 1967.

Table 6.3
Index numbers of wholesale prices
Base 1952-53 = 100

Main Groups

Groups	Weight	(Financial Year Average)			
		1950-51	1955-56	1960-61	1965-66
All commodities	1000	110.8	92.5	124.9	165.1
Food articles	504	112.5	86.6	120.0	168.8
Foodgrains	235	94.2	73.1	102.3	150.3
Liquor and tobacco	21	98.4	81.0	109.9	136.6
Fuel, power, light and lubricants	30	92.6	95.2	120.0	153.0
Industrial raw materials	155	130.9	99.0	145.4	189.1
Manufactures	290	103.3	99.7	123.9	149.2
Intermediate products	41	112.4	100.1	130.6	172.3
Finished products	249	101.8	99.6	122.8	145.4

Source:

Annual Reports on Currency and Finance, Reserve
Bank of India, 1965-66.

From a study of the above statistical representa-
tions, a number of conclusions emerge:
1. Price level registered a basic upward trend
   during the second and third plans.
2. Rise in the wholesale prices by about 48 percent
   during the first three plans may be divided into
   four distinct phases.
   2.1 In the phase covering the period of the
       first plan prices declined by 17.3 percent.
   2.2 In the second phase covering the period of
       the second plan prices rose by 35 percent.
   2.3 In the third phase of the third plan cover-
       ing first two years, prices were relatively
       stable (Table 6.2) rising by only 1.2
       percent a year.
   2.4 In the last phase covering the last three
       years of the third plan annual rate of rise
       far exceeded that of the preceding ten years
       or that of the three plan periods.

3. The spearhead of price rise rested in food
   articles and raw materials. Excepting raw
   materials during the second plan, the rise was
   the largest in the group 'food articles' which
   play the crucial role in the general price movement. Industrial raw materials also rose more
   than food articles during the last three years
   of the third plan (Table 6.2).
4. Intermediate products rose more than manufactures
   and finished products during the latter two plans,
   the last two groups registering more or less
   equal percentage rise.

It is thus apparent that there was manifest, during
the second and third plan-periods, a general and
continual rising trend in the average and group price-
levels. This phenomenon apart, there were a few other
characteristic features of the price spiral.

Firstly, the hitherto seasonal character of prices
started, for the first time, disappearing, particularly
in respect of agricultural products, and, as a result
(Table 6.4) the seasonal rise and fall in prices gave
way to a new trend of continual price rise.

This phenomenon is attributable to shortfalls in
domestic output and decline in market arrivals resulting
in smaller seasonal declines in the post-harvest period,
availability through imports and release from government
stocks dampening price rise in the lean season, and
better storage and marketing facilities in the producing
centres.

Surprisingly, however, while government control and
market-participation dampened seasonal price-movements,
they did not lead to a downward trend in prices in the
rest of the markets. It would be like playing an ostrich
if we fail to assess the correct reason for this phenomenon. Hoarding and regulated black market supply also
largely did away with seasonality of prices and stabi-
lised price-rise at high plateaus.

Secondly, prices showed stickiness. Earlier, prices
used to rise and fall in response to a bumper crop or a
season of drought with crop failures, or with large scale
imports. Not so any more (Table 6.5). A cumulative rise
in prices was the result of the narrowing down of
seasonal movement in prices and of their stickiness, as
we may call it.

Despite all the efforts at industrialisation, the
framework of the economy continued to remain agronomic.
Agricultural prices, therefore, played a major role in
the up-key or down-key movements of the general price
level. The information presented in Table 6.6 amply
illustrates the part played by agricultural prices; how
these by their direct contribution to the corresponding
movement in the general prices indirectly through rise in

Table 6.4
Average amplitudes of seasonal indices (percentages)

Period (financial year)	All commodities	Food articles	Cereals	Pulses	Industrial raw materials	Raw cotton	Raw jute	Groundnuts
1951-56	4.1	7.4	7.3	10.0	2.5	4.5	14.8	14.6
1956-61	3.9	7.4	7.1	8.3	2.0	4.3	8.0	13.8
1961-66	3.9	7.6	6.7	9.0	2.1	3.9	4.9	13.1

Source:

R.B.I. Bulletin, June 1965 and June 1967.

Table 6.5
Seasonal variations (percentages) in wholesale price
index during 1961-62 to 1965-66
Base 1952-53 = 100

Period	All commodities	Food articles	Cereals	Pulses	Industrial raw materials
1961a	+ 4.2	+ 8.2	+ 5.0	+ 4.3	+ 0.5
1961-62b	- 5.8	- 6.4	- 3.5	+ 1.4	-12.6
1962a	+ 7.0	+11.9	+ 7.9	+21.2	+ 3.5
1962-63b	- 2.9	- 6.3	- 6.3	-11.3	- 3.2
1963a	+ 7.8	+13.4	+14.1	+10.2	+ 5.3
1963-64b	- 2.7	- 3.8	+ 0.8	+ 7.8	- 3.9
1964a	+19.9	+27.7	+29.5	+55.5	+25.8
1964-65b	- 6.1	-11.1	- 8.4	-16.2	- 5.6
1965a	+11.3	+14.7	+ 9.0	+10.8	+15.5
1965-66b	+ 3.9	- 0.3	+ 3.5	-11.7	+12.3

Source:

R.B.I. Bulletin, June 1967.

Note:

a - lean season generally covering the period
March to August of a year.
b - period of seasonal decline generally covering
August to March (of the following year).

Table 6.6
Weighted percentage variations

Commodity group	Percent weighted variations			Percent contribution to rise or fall in overall index		
	I Plan	II Plan	III Plan	I Plan	II Plan	III Plan
Agricultural commodities	-12.3	+12.1	+18.1	71.1	60.1	56.3
Agriculture-based commodities	- 4.4	+10.9	+ 9.9	25.4	31.0	30.7
Non-agricultural commodities	- 0.6	+ 3.1	+ 4.2	3.5	8.9	13.0
General Index	-17.3	+35.1	+32.2	100.0	100.0	100.0

Source:

R.B.I. Bulletin, June 1967.

Table 6.7
Combined index of price-regulated items

	1961-62	1962-63	1963-64	1964-65	1965-66
1. Price-regulated items					
Index	120.8	125.1	132.7	130.0	144.8
Weight	111.0	111.0	129.0	362.0	362.0
Change in index	-	+3.0	+6.1	+4.7	+4.2
2. Non-regulated items					
Index	125.6	128.2	135.7	160.5	176.6
Weight	889.0	889.0	871.0	638.0	638.0
Change in index	-	+2.1	+5.9	+18.3	+10.0

industrial wages influenced prices of a whole range of
non-agricultural commodities.

Fourthly, the trends in prices of commodities, which
are controlled or regulated, might be referred to as
another important feature of the price movements particularly during the third plan... With the increasing
shortages of supplies in relation to demand the continuous pressure since 1963-64 on prices of essential items,
the number of price-controlled or regulated items was

progressively increased during 1963-64 to 1965-66.[23]

Here, the active role played by the black market operations and the compelling negative forces unleashed by black money, made the price spiral frolic up with more sensitive vibration than expected. They cashed in on all controls of commodities, regulations of prices, as also on the shortages in supplies and unsatisfied demand in the market.[24]

Table 6.7 shows that the weight of the price regulated items more than trebled and in the last year of the third plan was nearly one-third of the total weight of the index. In this connection it was stated that the extent of rise in prices of regulated items was much less than in the case of non-regulated items. It was difficult to indicate how effective price-control was in ensuring a smaller rise in the prices of the regulated items... On the other hand, the indices of price-regulated items, based as they were on official prices, might not reflect the effective price level. Therefore, the price rise experienced in the last three years, 1963-64 to 1965-66, were in the nature of marginally repressed inflation.[25]

Table 6.8 manifested a basic imbalance between aggregate supply and aggregate demand indicating the persistent rise in the general price level from the second plan. Table 6.9 highlights imbalances of supply showing percentage change in output.

There was thus a declining trend in the production of foodgrains. It was not only to arrest possibilities of acute scarcity in certain states, but also to prevent the prices of foodgrains from catapulting that the fall in food-output was continually supported by large-scale imports.

The share of imports of foodgrains to the supply was 2.6 percent in the first plan, 49 percent in the second plan and 7.5 percent in the third plan.

In the case of non-food articles also, particularly raw cotton and raw jute, imports during the third plan were larger than during the second plan. But for imports, the rise in prices of agricultural output would have been even greater.[26]

Prices of industrial output

Overall growth, apart from distribution, has a major role to play in the fluctuation of prices of agri-cultural commodities, particularly foodgrains and cereals. It is, however, to some extent, different in case of industrial output. More than the overall growth as such, it is the relative growth of the components that has the largest impact on their prices. Then again the prices of consumer goods and non-consumer goods showed a tendency of averaging out at a higher level by the activities of the general market, according to the

Table 6.8 Imbalance between supply
and demand
(In percent)

Particulars	I Plan	II Plan	III Plan
(a) Growth in net national expenditure at market price	+ 6	+44	+50
(b) Growth in net national output at constant prices	+18	+22	+14
(c) Change in wholesale prices (1952-53 = 100)	-17	+35	+32.2

Source:

R.B.I. Bulletin, June 1967.

Table 6.9 Percentage change in output

	Agriculture			Industry				
	Food	Non-food	Total	Basic goods	Capital goods	Inter-mediate goods	Cons-umer goods	Total
	a	b	a+b	c	d	e	f	c+d+e+f
I Plan	+27.4	+13.2	22.2	N.A.	N.A.	N.A.	N.A.	26.0
II Plan	+18.9	+27.3	21.7	+67.2	+50.1	+21.3	+14.7	+30.8
III Plan	-11.5	- 0.1	-7.4	+55.0	+98.1	+36.0	+28.7	+38.7

Source:

R.B.I. Bulletin, June 1967.

laws of demand and supply, while uncertainties are
created in the range of prices in such products by the
activities of the black marketeer.

Comparatively lower rate of growth of consumption
goods in the second and third plans contributed to the
rise in the general price level despite a considerable
growth in non-consumer goods. The imbalance of the same
factors again became manifest from around the middle of
the fourth five year plan.

Commodity speculation and black marketing have been
two major factors responsible for hoarding, commodity-
fadeouts and price-hikes in industrial outputs throughout
the plans, such phenomena becoming more proficient from
around the middle of second plan, when investment markets

became tight, and again during the course of the third
and fourth plans whenever the supply became lean and
controls and price schedules were imposed by the
government.[27] The modus operandi of the black marketeer
in this respect has been surveyed at length in chapter 2
of the present treatise.

Decline in the percentage share of import in
national output during the third plan contributed to the
spurt in price rise. Severe import restrictions owing
to persistent foreign exchange difficulties and availability of the bulk of the foreign aid for import of
investment goods diverted the pressure of demand to
domestic output,and of total availability in the context
of planned growth,impaired under the price level from
the supply side.[28]

This is a very important factor to take note of.
Whenever there is a fall in supply, government makes
efforts to make up the leeway by large-scale imports.
But due to foreign exchange difficulties, imports had
to be controlled. On the other hand, exports which earn
foreign exchange could not be boosted up further due to
overall shortage in domestic supply. After a few years
of favourable balance of payments, the position on the
exchange counter has again become strained.

Factors relating to demand

Factors which operated on the demand side have
been:

1. Increase of population;
2. Comparative increase in employment and income;
3. Urbanisation;
4. Rise in government expenditure; and
5. Monetary expansion.

We shall examine these factors individually.

Throughout the plan period, population explosion
continued unabated. The annual average rate of growth
of population was 2.2 percent and 3 percent respectively
during 1951-61 and 1961-65. This continued demographical
upsurge, coupled with overall shortage in supply, made
more difficult by hoarding, supply fadeouts, cornering
and such other devices of the black market, reacted very
heavily on the current supplies of wage goods and
services. Too many people were competing with far too
restricted a supply. Whereas, in the agricultural and
private sectors, under-employment as also disguised and
absolute unemployment continued, there were, as a
consequence of the plan-investments and expansions,
steady rise in employment and income in mines and
factories (Table 6.10) and in the public sector (Table
6.11). The result of this trend was obvious, as 'a
large part of the incomes generated in the public and
private sectors has been in the form of wages and has
accrued to those sections of the population whose

Table 6.10
Indices of employment and money wages

Period	Employment (1951=100)		Money Wages Per Worker (1951=100)	
	Factories	Mines	Factories	Mines
I Plan (1951-56)	103.4 (+1.5)	104.4 (+2.0)	107.2 (+3.1)	106.0 (+2.5)
II Plan (1956-60)	123.2 (+3.8)	116.8 (+2.1)	121.4 (+2.9)	169.6 (+11.9)
III Plan (1961-64)	144.8 (+4.9)	125.0 (+1.3)	144.0 (+3.8)	210.8 (+3.8)

Source:

Indian Labour Statistics, 1966.
N.B. Brackets indicate annual rates of increase.

Table 6.11
Employment and income in the public sector

End of	Employment*		Income generated*		
	Mill-ions per-cent	Percent increase	Period	Rs.in crores	Percent increase
March 1951	N.A.	...	1950-51	339.6	...
March 1956	5.2	...	1955-56	426.6	+ 25.6
March 1961	7.1	+36.5	1960-61	615.0	+ 44.2
March 1966	9.4	+32.4	1965-66	1232.3	+100.4

* Includes public sector and through budgetary operations of the Central Government.

Source:

Economic Survey, 1966-67 and R.B.I. Bulletin, June 1967.

propensity to consume is high'.

Growth of factory employment and income led to greater urbanisation. Rate of growth per annum of urban population during the three plans was, as brought out by the 1971 census results, successively 2.4, 2.8 and 5.1.[29] Rates of growth of total population, rural population and urban population in the decade 1951-61 were 21.64, 20.77, 26.41 and in the decade 1961-71 were 24.66, 21.78

and 37.89 respectively.

The tendency to increasing urbanisation has been vividly illustrated in a Supplement to the 1971 Census Results indicated by the growth in the number of towns and their population growth rate in India. The trends have been indicated in Table 6.12.

Fourthly, substantial rise in government expenditure, particularly during the third plan, contributed heavily to the expansion of monetary demand. While this aspect of the matter and its repercussion on the price fluctuations and inflationary trends will be discussed at greater length later in chapter 7, Table 6.13 indicates the magnitude of this factor.

Finally, increasing net national expenditure required a crucial support. This consisted in monetary expansion contributing to the generation of inflationary pressures. This is what has been generally described as deficit financing. Table 6.14 suggests that in this process money supply was a more important variable than velocity.[30] This also deserves a fuller treatment, and will, therefore, be examined later in some depth.

The phenomenon may be summarised as under:

1. Expansion in monetary resources during the three plan periods was largely due to the increase in government sectors' indebtedness to the banking system, mainly to the Reserve Bank. Net bank credit to government showed a larger rise than that to private sector during the first and second plans. In the third plan, however, bank credit to private sector increased by 77 percent compared with a rise of 61 percent in respect of public sector.
2. Public sector's expenditure, both development and non-development, was carried on in the face of difficulties of resource mobilisation arising from low ratio of savings in the economy.
3. In order, therefore, to solve the problem of availability of financial resources, the government resorted to inflationary financing through Reserve Bank credit.
4. Similarly, increasing reliance of the private sector on bank credit suggested that savings within the private sector fell short of expenditure, and that resort to bank credit by this sector also added to the pressures on price level generated by public expenditure.[31]

Sectional prices

It is infrequently appreciated that the trends in wholesale prices and general price index is a compound of developments in the price ranges of individual or group prices. These are called sectional prices for specific or groups of commodities. These prices

82

Table 6.12 Trends of increasing urbanisation

| | Number of towns | | | Growth rate of population | |
	1951	1961	1971	1951-61	1961-71
Class I (100,000)+	81	113	142	+44.47	+49.35
Class II (50,000 to 99,999)	102	138	198	+39.26	+40.86
Class III (20,000 to 49,999)	353	484	617	+40.14	+29.10
Class IV (10,000 to 19,999)	630	748	931	+18.23	+27.30
Class V (5,000 to 9,999)	1,158	760	756	-30.07	-00.09
Class VI (less than 5,000)	599	218	277	-62.30	+16.18
All classes				+26.41	+37.83

Source:

Census of India, 1971, Paper I of 1971 Supplement.

Table 6.13 Government expenditure, net national expenditure, and net national income

| Period | Government expenditure | Net national expenditure (a)(Rs. in average | Net national income (b) | Percentage of column 1 to | |
| | | | | column 2 | column 3 |
	1	2	3	4	5
I Plan (1951-56)	10.3	105.7	99.7	9.7	10.3
II Plan (1956-61)	17.5 (8.7)	134.5 (7.6)	124.8 (7.3)	13.0	14.0
III Plan (1961-65)	31.0 (18.3)	172.3 (18.2)	168.9 (9.2)	...	...

Source:

Estimates of National Income, C.S.O. Budget documents; R.B.I. Bulletin, June 1967.

Note:(a) At market prices   (b) At current prices
Figures in brackets represent annual rate of increase.

Table 6.14 <u>Trends of deficit financing</u> (In percent)

	I Plan March 1951-55	II Plan March 1956-61	III Plan March 1961-66
(a) Growth in net national expenditure (Market prices)	+ 6	+44	+50a
(b) Growth in monetary resources bcd	+14	+44	+60
(c) Increase in net bank credit to government d	+37	+125	+61
Private sector	+41	+81	+77

Source:

R.B.I. Bulletin, June 1967.

Note: a = Estimated.   b = Last Friday of March.
c = Currency plus aggregate deposits with banks.
d = Adjusted for P.L. 480 and P.L. 665 funds.

sometimes move in opposite directions, and sometimes movement in one reacts as a multiplier for another. These movements indicate the vital signals for formulation and implementation of policy.[32]

Substantial and continuous rise in the price of foodgrains (cereals and pulses) during the second and third plans indicated in Table 6.15 was the compound of result of growth in population and incomes, both rural and urban (the latter requiring steadily rising marketable surplus), the combined effect of which on demand is brought out in Table 6.16.

The demand for foodgrains had risen at the rate of about 3.7 percent per annum over the three plans whereas domestic output grew at the rate of about 2.4 percent per annum throughout the period. The forces of hoarding, cornering of supply and price-jumping in the black market is clearly evident as a constant undercurrent.[33]

A major factor sparking off price-rises has been the steadily growing gap between demand and supply, with a resultant mounting increase in the percentage of imports to total supply (Table 6.17). Apart from this, foodgrains prices were considerably influenced by short-term fluctuations of output owing to low price elasticity of demand. The gap between these was oftener than not artificially created by manoeuvres in the black market.[34]

Variability of market arrivals has more influence on prices than variability of production. The third plan recorded a steady decline in the percentage of market

Table 6.15
Present variation in wholesale prices of food articles
Base 1952-53 = 100

Groups	Weight	During			Annual average	
		First Plan	Second Plan	Third Plan	Second Plan	Third Plan
Food articles	504	-23.0	+38.6	+40.7	+ 6.9	+ 7.2
Foodgrains	235	-22.4	+39.9	+47.1	+ 6.96	+ 8.2
Cereals	(38.2)	-20.0	+36.8	+42.3	+ 7.2	+ 7.5
Rice	(22.4)	-17.0	+38.5	+30.6	+ 7.0	+ 5.6
Wheat	(10.6)	-24.2	+25.0	+53.4	+ 5.3	+ 9.5
Jawar	(1.9)	-26.3	+81.4	+61.8	+16.7	+12.9
Bajra	(1.0)	-12.3	+55.4	+46.5	+10.5	+ 8.7
Pulses	(8.4)	-32.2	+49.4	+74.1	+ 9.5	+12.8
Fruits & vegetables	(4.5)	- 5.4	+17.7	+48.9	+ 3.5	+ 8.8
Milk & ghee	(16.7)	-12.8	+29.5	+42.1	+ 5.4	+ 7.4
Edible oils	(9.3)	-42.4	+77.2	+55.8	+13.4	+10.0
Fish, eggs and meat	(3.4)	- 0.4	+28.9	+61.5	+ 5.3	+10.2
Sugar	(3.5)	- 4.9	+34.7	+20.6	+ 6.3	+ 3.9
Jagree	(6.0)	-55.6	+57.9	+18.7	+10.6	+ 6.5

Source:

Report on Currency and Finance, 1967-68
Statement 12; and R.B.I. Bulletin; June 1967.

Note:Brackets indicate percentage to the main group.

Table 6.16   Income and demand

	Indices (1950-51 = 100)				
	Per capita income	Income effect	Popula- tion effect	Combined effect	Total demand on the basis of col.4(mill- ion tonnes)
	1	2	3	4	5
1955-56	108.2	104.9	109.5	114.9	67.9
1960-61	118.7	111.2	121.6	135.2	81.7
1964-65	128.1	116.9	131.0	153.1	97.3

Source:
    R.B.I. Bulletin, June 1967.
Note: Column 2 is arrived at by assuming an elasticity

of demand of 0.6 for foodgrains. Column 3 is
based on the population growth rate of about
2 percent up to 1955-56 and about 24 percent for
the subsequent periods. Column 5 is arrived at
by applying the indices in column 4 to average
availability during 1953-56 which is assumed to be
equal to demand, as during this period there were
no controls and there was a decline in prices.

Table 6.17
Deficit in foodgrains (annual averages, million tonnes)

	Esti-mated demand	Pro-duc-tion	Gap (1-2) (Defi-cit)	Im-ports	Avail-ability	Imports as percentage of avail-ability
	1	2	3	4	5	6
I Plan (1951-56)	65.3	65.8	+0.5	1.8	67.6	2.6
II Plan (1956-61)	75.5	75.2	-0.3	3.9	79.1	4.9
III Plan (1961-66)	90.3	80.5	-9.8	6.5	87.0	7.5

Source:
    R.B.I. Bulletin, June 1967.

Table 6.18
Percentage of market arrivals to marketable surplus

Period	Rice	Wheat	Jawar
1960-61	11.5	11.1	8.9
1961-62	11.8	9.8	7.6
1962-63	12.2	11.9	7.3
1963-64	8.4	12.4	6.5
1964-65	6.9	7.5	4.2
1965-66	7.2	8.7	4.9

Source:

    R.B.I. Bulletin, June 1967.
    Market survey conducted in chapter 2 of the
    present treatise.

arrivals to marketable surplus as shown in Table 6.18.
This characteristic[35] is due to:
1. State purchases and procurements;
2. The increased tendency on the part of large and
   medium farmers to withhold supplies from the
   market in anticipation of rising prices;
3. Increased consumption in rural areas owing to
   favourable trends in agricultural income;
4. Interrelationship among various cereals in
   regard to output, market arrivals and prices; and
5. Downright hoarding and black marketing in
   cereals.

The compound effect of all these on market arrivals
is shown in Table 6.18.

The invisible shadow

At every stage of the market arrivals, non-arrivals
and price jumping in India, however, right through the
plan periods, the invisible influence of black market,
operated by black money, has been elongating the price-
hikes and very often stabilising them at what may be
called Pamir plateaus of price-rise.

These forces have been procuring and cornering
supplies, withholding investible surplus and generally
inhibiting growth and spreading and maintaining in
distribution of the national product, an element of
inequality and freezing of wealth.

Investment

Development under organised state planning in the
Indian situation brought about a growing rate of investment from not only resource mobilisation but also deficit
financing and debt servicing. It was necessary, to
forestal price-rises, to counterbalance such growing
investment with larger savings.

The first impact of growing money incomes due to
increased investment in an under-developed country is
on foodgrains prices caused by unbalanced growth of
agriculture and industry. During the first, second and
third plans, the percentage growth of agricultural output
throughout was at a tangent, so to say, with that of
industrial output.

Conclusion

Many factors, starting from certain compelling
considerations of plan strategy, effects of wars,
draughts and crop failures, to debt servicing, diminishing returns on import and less favourable exchange
balances, therefore, have been responsible for galloping
price spiral since independence. But one major decideratum has been the forces unleashed by black market, black
money and national and international smuggling and
drainage in foreign exchange resources.

NOTES
    1. S.K. Ray - Fundamental Disequilibrium, Inflation
and Devaluation; Business Standard, Calcutta, May 31,1975.
    2. S.K. Ray - This Inflationary Decade; Business
Standard, Calcutta, April 18 & 19, 1977.
    3. First Five Year Plan; Planning Commission,
Government of India.
    4. Graeme Dorrace - Inflation and Growth; The
Statistical Evidence; I.M.F. Staff Papers; March 1966.
    5. Geoffrey Manyard - Economic Development and
the Price Level.
    6. Economic Development with Stability; A Report
to the Government of India, 1954.
    7. S.K. Ray - This Inflationary Decade; Business
Standard, Calcutta, April 18 & 19, 1977.
    8. S.K. Ray - Inflation As An Economic Phenomenon;
Financial Express, Bombay, June 28 & 29, 1979.
    9. S.K. Ray - This Inflationary Decade; Business
Standard, Calcutta, April 18 & 19, 1977.
    10. J.J. Anjaria - Reserve Bank of India Bulletin;
January 1969.
    11. Ibid.
    12. Chapter 3 of the present study.
    13. Anjaria - Reserve Bank of India Bulletin;
January 1969.
    14. Ibid.
    15. Final Report of Direct Taxes Enquiry Committee,
1971.
    16. S.K. Ray - Economics of Black Market Profits;
Economic Times, New Delhi, November 25, 1974.
    17. S.K. Ray - India's Balance of Payments;
Business Standard, Calcutta, March 4 & 5, 1978.
    18. Reserve Bank of India Bulletin; January 1969.
    19. Index Number of Wholesale Prices in India
(Revised Series), week ending April 14, 1956; Government
of India.
    20. Anjaria - Reserve Bank of India Bulletin;
January 1969.
    21. Velayudhan - Reserve Bank of India Bulletin;
January 1969.
    22. J. Stafford - Indices of Wholesale Prices;
Journal of the Royal Statistical Society, 1969.
    23. Annual Report on Currency & Finance, 1967-68,
Reserve Bank of India.
    24. Chapter 2 of the present study.
    S.K. Ray - Economics of Black Market Profits;
Economic Times, New Delhi, November 25, 1974.
    25. Ibid (21)
    26. Percentage of merchandise imports to net national
output:
        I Plan   + 7.3
        II Plan + 8.5

88

III Plan   + 7.0

27. S.K. Ray - Economics of Black Market Profits;
Economic Times, New Delhi; November 25,1974.

28. Ibid (21).

29. S.S. Madalgi - Population and Food Supply in
India; Lalvani Publishing House; New Delhi, 1970.

30. Liquidity in the Indian Economy; R.B.I. Bulletin,
November 1963.

31. Velayudhan - Reserve Bank of India Bulletin;
June 1967.

32. Ibid.

33. S.K. Ray - Economics of Black Market; Eastern
Economist, June 21, 1968.

34. Ibid.

35. Annual Report on Currency & Finance, 1967-68;
Reserve Bank of India.

7

Prices, Inflation, and Money Supply

Hand in hand with the price spiral move the curves of inflation and money supply, or vice versa. In modern development-economics, no other problem has assumed greater importance than the triumvirate rise of prices, inflation and money supply.

Expanding government control over economic activity has characterised life in the twentieth century... The forces pressing for greater government intervention in economic life are fundamental and lie deep in the socio-economic structure of different countries.[1]

In this expanding role of government control in the economy, nothing else is more important today in the Indian situation than the three problems of price-spiral, galloping inflation and an expanding base of currency circulation impinging on both prices and inflation.

A world-wide phenomenon

Inflation, as an economic malaise, is no more confined to any single country. Nor is it any more a unique phenomenon peculiar to the developing economies of South East Asia and Latin America, as it used to be a decade ago. Inflation is today lashing the economies of both underdeveloped and advanced countries, no matter whether such economies have a production-glut or serious shortage in supply.

In the recent twelve months ending March 1975, for which the United Nations have compiled statistical information, the price level in the United Kingdom soared by 13.5 percent, in France by 12.2 percent and in Japan by 25 percent. In India, the rate of inflation for six months ending March 1975 has been 25 percent. The system of economy has ceased to be of any validity as far as inflation is concerned. While Greece has a 33 percent annual growth of inflation, Switzerland had 12 and Yugoslavia 22 percent.[2] (Diagram at page 102).

Two factors have catapulted inflation as the most important international economic problem:

1. The range of economic inequity expands under the influence of inflation. This favours specula-tion vis-a-vis lawful investment and weakens the distribution system.
2. Remedial strategies so far tried in India and abroad, e.g. commodity controls and rationing, price ceiling and freezing, rigorous public finance and lighter credit, have proved no panacea, and financial experts have found no straight or lasting solution.

Irving Friedman is of the opinion that inflation in most part of the world has come in reversal of the cycle of depression to today's affluence. The depression of the 'thirties goaded the governments in Europe and America to implement policies which catered for full employment.

But this policy appears to have turned a complete circle, engaging the governments in huge expenses in service departments and in paying for education, health, social security and even employment. The overhead of affluence, as we may call it, has turned out to be too costly. Besides, the forces of international economics and the burden of growth in the developing economies, all created situations under which growth, with higher wages and costlier investment, tended to raise prices.

A series of crop failures in 1972, caused by phenomenally foul weather round the world, aggravated shortages of wheat, maize, soyabeans and even fodder. Oil countries also whipped up prices of oil and soared up production-costs and thereby inflation.[3]

One thing led to another, and finally we have a situation when almost all the economies in the world are chasing spiralling inflation. The situation has become more acute in certain developing economies, and more than most in the Indian situation which is replete with investment financed by deficit money supply, tighter credit, vagaries of demand and supply and machinations of the black market and forces of the black money.[4]

Indexing

Economists have considered several strategies to arrest global inflation. One solution advocated by several prominent economists and given a trial in varying degrees and different ways in Brazil, Canada and Europe, is indexing - that is, raising or lowering incomes, taxes, savings or even debts in line with price trends. In theory, this arrangement would preserve real incomes and purchasing power. In practice, it has failed in varying degrees in different countries like Brazil.

Other strategies being considered and experimented with are the following:[5]

1. Concerted action to expand world food production.
2. Creation of a world commodities union for effective distribution between different parts of the world.
3. Reformation of trade practices, by tearing down artificial barriers to world trade.
4. Depressing demand adequate enough to bring prices down.

No concrete and decisive strategy to correct world inflation has as yet been agreed upon, not even by the economists attached to the International Monetary Fund and the World Bank. The situation is rather confused and indeterminate.

Inflationary pressure

The inflationary pressure in the Indian economy is illustrated by Table 6.14 in chapter 6. Evidence of inflationary pressure during the second and third plans has been noted earlier. Growth of plan outlay by 138 percent during the second plan was accompanied by 15 percent rise in foodgrains prices and about 39 percent rise in the prices of food articles.

During the third plan, price rate of food articles was more or less the same as in the second plan, but foodgrains prices rose by 57 percent in spite of the rate of growth of the plan outlay being half that of the second plan.

By this time the inflationary pressure on prices had caught on the multiplier effect. Growth in output and import availability kept the rise in price of food-grains in the second plan lower than in the third, which bore the impact of diminution of output not sufficiently counteracted by import availability.[6]

Inflation reduced the real content of investment resulting in shortfall of output targets. The average annual increase of aggregate investment during the three plans at current prices and at 1948-49 prices were respectively 21.7, 14.4, 9.7 and 24.5, 10.7 and 4.2 respectively.

The delay in fulfilment of investment plans being equivalent to a lengthening of the gestation period of investment, the check to inflation (in the shape of large supplies) was weakened. Moreover, the price rise resulted in a diversion of resources to those forms of investment on which there is scope for larger capital gains, viz., gold, land, urban house property and commodities experiencing price rises.[7]

Did savings respond to the growing demand of investment? Answer to this can be worked out from an analysis of Table 7.1. A scrutiny of this table brings out the following features:

1. Throughout the period individuals contributed the

Table 7.1
National saving (net) estimates

(Rs. crores)

	At current prices				At 1948-49 prices			
	1950-51	1955-56	1960-61	1964-65	1950-51	1955-56	1960-61	1964-65
Indivi-duals	500 (79.2)	996 (87.0)	1058 (75.1)	1126 (84.7)	534 (79.2)	1046 (87.0)	952 (75.1)	844 (84.7)
Corpo-rate	32 (4.3)	39 (3.4)	122 (8.6)	127 (9.5)	31 (4.3)	41 (3.4)	100 (8.6)	96 (9.5)
Govern-ment	120 (16.8)	109 (9.6)	288 (16.3)	75 (5.8)	110 (16.5)	115 (9.6)	205 (16.3)	56 (5.8)
Total	732 (100)	1144 (100)	1408 (100)	1328 (100)	675 (100)	1022 (100)	1267 (100)	996 (100)

Source:

Saving in India During the Plan Periods, NCAER, June 1966.

bulk (above 75 percent) of the savings of the
economy.
2. Aggregate savings diminished (in absolute amount)
during the third plan.
3. Fall of savings was the largest in the government sector.
4. Compared to the first plan, the absolute growth
of savings of the individual sector was very low
during the second and third plans.
   Fall in the rate of savings during the third plan
is partly due to the lower rate of growth of income.
Part of the explanation is the higher rate of consumption,
especially of the public sector, through increasing
investment in public sector undertakings and inadequate
stress on curbing non-developmental expenditure. A
further explanation may be that a redistribution of
income has taken place from the relatively saving group
to the relatively consuming group.
   While rising prices affect voluntary savings
adversely, in an underdeveloped country like India the
inflationary process itself originates a savings
deficit. In underdeveloped countries the level of real
income being low, voluntary savings by the community
through a reduction in consumption are not sufficient
to finance investment required for the growth of per
capita real income... The gap between the required
investment and available savings is filled by the
government through creation of additional money. However,
such creation of money, though it initially diverts
resources into investment, would after a point lead to a

situation where there are not enough resources available
to meet the enlarged money demand except at higher
prices.[8]

Yet another important factor which impinged on
investible surplus and led to tighter investment and
inflation is unaccounted money. This has been brought
out in great detail in the Report of the Direct Taxes
Enquiry Committee, 1971. The extent of black money in
the economy, and the role played by black money in
flight of resources and thereupon in tighter credit and
investment situation, which injected the price spiral
with an inflationary fever, has been discussed at length
in chapter 3 of the present study.

The pattern has been a consistently rising trend
in prices. Thus, to recapitulate from chapter 6, wholesale prices rose by 22 percent in 1972-73, and by another
28 percent the following year. In 1974-75, it rose by
another 17 percent. There is little consolation that
the percentage rise has been comparatively lesser in
1974-75, when it is remembered that each year's rise has
been cumulative. Due to the multiplier effect on prices,
the cost of living has gone up by about 75 percent in
this three-year period. This, coupled with crop failures,
hoarding and rabid inflation, has been very rough on
the average consumer.

There has been a drop in prices in 1975. The downward trend in wholesale prices was however temporary and
inflation has not really been brought under control on
any long-term pattern. The wholesale price index by
March 1975 had registered a steady fall in preceding
six months.[9] This has been followed by a rise of 10
percent in three months and another 0.15 percent in
three subsequent months in the prices of essential
commodities.[10]

To bring up the analysis on the trend of the Indian
inflation to date, it is marked by a high annual rate of
21.2 percent registered by the end of July 1980.

Sugar prices went up by a colossal 126.8 percent,
potatoes by 69.9 percent, fish by 65.5 percent, meat by
26.3 percent, while gram by 53.5 percent, rice by 16.1
percent, wheat by 8.5 percent and mustard oil by 31.8
percent. These disturbing portents, particularly in
food-articles, have been reflected in the latest official
analysis on the Indian price spiral.[11]

Two factors vitally responsible for price fluctuations are money supply and agricultural production. The
former is determined by fiscal and monetary policy. The
latter in India still depends largely on the monsoon.
Other factors such as speculation, hoarding, smuggling,
a rise in the international prices of imported goods
and so on are also important, but rather as subsidiary
factors, which however frequently assume great importance.

Money supply

Beginning with 1969-70 there was a sharp annual
increase in money supply till March 1974. In 1969-70
it was 10.8 percent more than in the previous year; it
was 11.2 percent in 1970-71, 13.1 percent in 1971-72,
15.9 percent in 1972-73 and 15.3 percent in 1973-74,
against the growth rate of national income of 5.7 percent,
4.9 percent, 1.4 percent, 0.9 percent and 3.1 percent
respectively.

An important section of post-Keynesian economists
believes that, if prices are to remain stable, the
growth rate of money supply should be kept close to the
growth rate of economy.

In India however the growth rate of money supply has
gone up sharply over the years when the increase in
national income has shown a downward trend. Thus in
1971-72, when the growth rate in national income fell
to 1.4 percent from the previous year's 4.9 percent,
the increase in money supply went up from 11.2 percent to
13.1 percent. The next year the situation was worse.
These trends were responsible, according to the Economic
Survey for 1975 Union Budget, for the unprecedented
economic strain in the history of independent India.

When the situation appeared to be getting serious,
certain quick-silver steps were taken. From July 1974
onward the government has taken a series of measures
to control credit and reduce budgetary deficits. Their
success in terms of the limited object of controlling
money supply can be seen from the fact that the growth
rate in the first ten months of 1974-75 was 3.1 percent
against 15.3 percent in the previous year.

The drive against smuggling and black money was
also launched, and the drive had an effect on the
parallel economy, at least for the time being, run by
speculators, hoarders, smugglers and profiteers.

The fall in wholesale prices started when black
money temporarily ceased to make speculative deals in
the commodity market. The steep rise in interest rates
affected inventory-piling in industry. Partly because
of the high price of credit demanded by banks, partly
due to the lowering of credit limits and partly because
of the falling trend in wholesale prices, which made
speculative build-up of inventories unnecessary and
unprofitable, producers made a drastic cut in their
stocks of raw materials and finished products.

The falling trend in prices, which slowly began in
October 1974, could not have been sustained if the rabi
crop in 1975 had not been good. While from all accounts,
the rabi has given a bumper harvest in 1973, the kharif
crop was not very encouraging, total production being
less than 60 million tonnes. The rabi crop was estimated
to be 44 million tonnes, making a total output of 704

million tonnes for the agricultural year 1974-75. This
is 4.8 million tonnes less than the record production of
180.6 million tonnes in 1970-71. The deficiency has been
made up, however, by importing around five million
tonnes. A sense of relief in the food situation also
helped to sustain the downward trend in prices for some
time.[12]

A seasonal fall in prices during December-May is
common. This is due to the kharif, and a little later
the rabi crop, coming into the market. From the middle
of May, prices begin to rise. In 1973-74, because of
the strong inflationary situation, the upward trend
continued even during the crop season. It was felt that
the old pattern of price changes had become untenable.
Actually, prices failed to fall during the 1973-74 crop
season because of inflation and black market and black
money fostering the same.

A few imponderables

What are the prospects of the Indian economy reaching a satisfactory level of production but counter-
inflationary level of stability? Will it be possible to
banish inflation from the Indian economy for, say, the
next fifty years? It is difficult to find answers to
these questions because there are several imponderables.

The first thing to be considered in this connection
is the trend in money supply. In March 1969 the total
money supply with the public was Rs.5,838 crores; by
March 1975 this had risen to Rs.11,546 crores. During
the same period real national product increased from
Rs.19,444 crores (at 1960-61 prices) to Rs.21,426 crores,
a rise of 10.2 percent in six years. Thus against a
growth rate in money supply of 13 percent the growth
rate of national income was no more than 1.4 percent a
year.

This trend was partially halted as a result of
strict fiscal and monetary discipline, for some time,
but not actually reversed. In fact, money supply
increased from Rs.10,848 crores in March 1974 to
Rs.11,343 crores on January 17, 1975, and Rs.11,546
crores on March 21, 1975. On March 28, it was slightly
lower at Rs.11,501 crores, which however marked an
increase of 6 percent over the figure for the corresponding week in 1974.[13]

Besides, a fundamental change has taken place over
the last few years in the composition of money supply.
Since 1961-62, the percentage of currency in the total
money supply has shown a declining trend. From 72.2
percent at the end of 1961-62 it declined to 62.1 percent
in the three years, 1968-69 to 1970-71, 58.5 percent
in the next three years, 1971-72 to 1973-74 and 55.7
percent in January 1975. The progressive decline in the
ratio of currency to money supply has resulted in raising

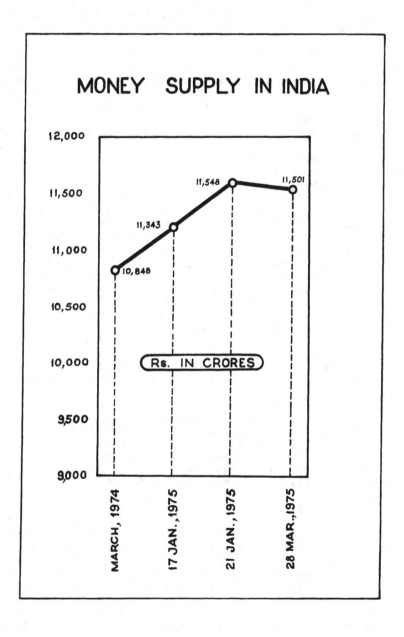

MONEY SUPPLY IN INDIA

Rs. IN CROMES

the value of money multiplier and this has increased the magnitude of expansionary impulses associated with any given level of deficit financing.[14]

The decline in the growth rate of money supply over the last one year to 6 percent is to be welcomed, but its potential for causing inflation is increasing, because of the rise in the value of money multiplier. The central budget for 1975-76 leaves uncovered a deficit of Rs.236 crores. This is Rs.100 crores more than the previous last year's budgeted deficit, and partly offsets the effect of the decline in the growth rate of money supply. Such a deficit together with an increase in the value of money multiplier would revive inflationary pressure as soon as the marketing of rabi and kharif crops is over. This started happening from mid-1975.

No one again can say for certain that the arrests of smugglers or black money operators made a lasting contribution; nor is it possible to measure the actual impact of the steps taken to impound a portion of the workers' increments. Both dividend control and compulsory deposits by income tax payers were peripheral to the problem of reducing purchasing power.

It has also to be seen how economic development takes shape with a change in government at New Delhi and the emphasis on the growth rate in future planning rather than on ad hoc economic developments and how the price spiral behaves with, God forbid, a failure of one or two monsoons.

It may be premature to say that the type of pressures and gooseberry-running strategies which often used to compel the two previous governments at the Centre adopt measures contrary to the current economic problems, have ceased to exist.[15] But now there is an apparent change in the government's attitude to growthmanship, which may be seen reflected even in the revision of the sixth Five Year Plan, since taken in hand by the Planning Commission of India.

The question is whether this new stress on stability will be carried to the point of subordinating the programme of economic revival to stability, though it is an integral part of stabilisation. It is not necessary to believe all that the Chambers of Commerce may say about the possibilities of recession; businessmen dislike any weakening of the sellers' market and may exaggerate the dangers of stagnation in an effort or to encourage the government to be bolder in fiscal policy.

It has been emphasised time and again that credit curbs should not be relaxed for the present because the inflationary pressure has not been fully contained. Could anti-inflationary monetary measures of 1974-75 succeed without the support of complementary fiscal measures? Nobody doubted the correctness of the

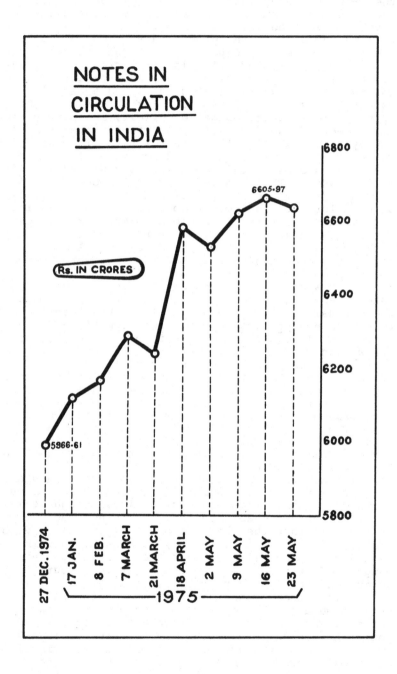

government policy in continuing monetary curbs under prevailing circumstances, but the contradictions in coupling that policy with continued budget deficit did give rise to certain misgivings. And, with a change in the government, even such measures were largely subjugated to sectoral economic interests and finally, during the regime of the interim government, to a virtual holiday in both monetary and fiscal anti-inflationary policy.[16]

Finally, the forces of black market, black money and smuggling at this stage again started marshalling their forces, and becoming gradually more effective. Certain decisions in courts of law also gave the smugglers a shot in the arm and the apparent hesitation by the subsequent governments at the Centre from mid-1977 to firmly put down economic offences including smuggling permanently, and not as a measure of temporary expedient, injected lot of uncertainty in the money, commodity and investment markets. The influence of the above forces on the price level was cancerous, and unless immediate, effective and permanent measures were taken to contain their manoeuvres, the price-level might develop into a nightmarish spiral. The latest official estimate already indicates a 21.2 percent annual inflation rate till the end of July 1980.

There is, however, hope for stability in prices, provided there is an increase in output, coupled with monetary discipline; these should help to raise the level of domestic savings besides releasing enough for development of resources. However, these will not by themselves guarantee the desired growth, but only make the conditions propitious for the success of fresh efforts for the implementation of development schemes forming a revised order of priorities in the sixth five year plan. Simultaneously, the need for both monetary and fiscal discipline along with an effective hunt for the forces of the black market and black money cannot be over-emphasised.

NOTES

1. Steiner - Government's Role In Economic Life; Mcgraw Hill Book Company, Inc.; New York, 1953.
2. Time, New York; April 8, 1974.
3. Reader's Digest; Bombay, August 1974.
4. S.K. Ray - Fundamental Disequilibrium, Inflation and Devaluation; Business Standard, Calcutta, May 31,1975.
5. Time, New York, April 8, 1974.
6. D.R. Khatkhate - The Impact of Inflation on India's Economic Development; Economic Development and Cultural Change; April 1969.
7. Estimates of Saving and Investment in Indian Economy; R.B.I. Bulletin, March 1965.

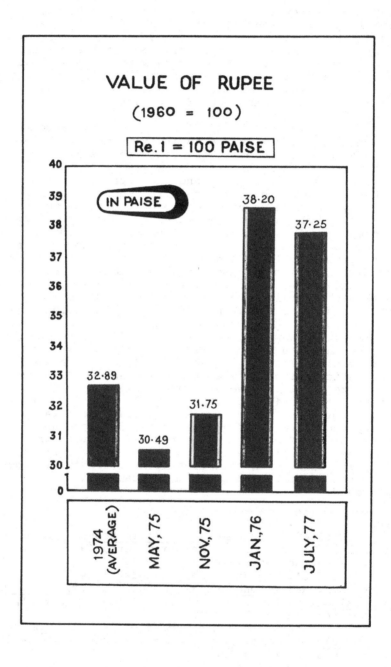

8. Ibid.

9. Calculated from Price Index Bulletins published by Government of India.

10. Inder Malhotra - The Illustrated Weekly of India, Bombay, April 3, 1977.

11. K.K. Sharma - The Statesman, New Delhi, August 21, 1980.

12. S.K. Ray - This Inflationary Decade; Business Standard, Calcutta, April 18 & 19, 1977.

Inder Malhotra - Illustrated Weekly of India; Bombay, April 3, 1977.

13. 1975 Economic Survey & General Budget Papers presented to the Indian Parliament.

14. Economic Survey for 1975 General Budget, presented to Indian Parliament.

15. Finance Commission Papers, 1974-75; 11 ibid.

16. A series of surveys on the health of the Indian economy, conducted by the Statesman, New Delhi, during 1975 and, again, during 1980.

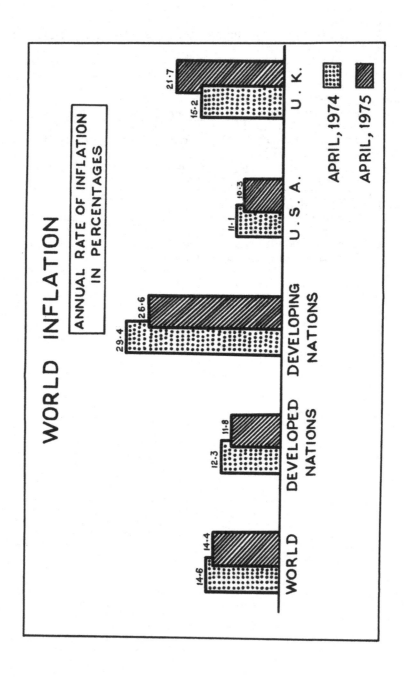

WORLD INFLATION

ANNUAL RATE OF INFLATION
IN PERCENTAGES

21·7
15·2
U. K.

10·3
11·1
U. S. A.

26·6
29·4
DEVELOPING
NATIONS

11·8
12·3
DEVELOPED
NATIONS

14·4
14·6
WORLD

APRIL, 1974

APRIL, 1975

8

Fraud, Misfeasance, and Jurisprudence

As techniques of operation, such activities as fraud and defalcation, embezzlement and misfeasance, are not exactly in the category of the black market. But as manifestations of distorted human behaviour, they are really not far removed. A discussion on frauds and other allied pursuits in the context of the present research is, therefore, relevant.

The scope of discussion in regard to fraud and misfeasance will be confined to public and private limited companies, public institutions and corporations and government departments. Almost all of these are governed by secretarial or directorial control and exposed to internal check and auditing. The position of the management and the auditor, particularly the auditor, vis-a-vis the organisation, and the role of statute and common laws and other branches of jurisprudence as possible checkmates for fraud and misfeasance, will also be considered at length.

The norms

The assets, including cash and investments of a company or a corporation or a government department are held and used by the management in the nature of a trust. The management holds the trust on behalf of the share-holders or the taxpayer, who are the beneficiaries.

As for all normal trusts, governed by the Indian Trusts Act, assets of a concern, both frozen and liquid, under the covenants of the trust, can be invested by the management only in furtherance of the interests of the beneficiaries, and nothing beyond the normal risks of prudent business investment are permissible, except by a referendum to the shareholders taken at a general body meeting, or in the case of a government department, without proper financial concurrence and administrative approval.

Nothing in the nature of wild-goose-chase should be undertaken by the management. In the name of

investment, the executive should not undertake what may
be known as racketeering or money jumping, all in the
nature of illegitimate speculation.

While this is one aspect, the other is that assets
including investments and cash should not be tampered
with, embezzled, defalcated, or even transferred to
another party without appropriate authorisation. These
will tantamount to a defrauding of the concern's
interests. Fraud is a phenomenon which an auditor is
to guard against as the watchdog of the shareholders or
the taxpayers. Fraud may include, apart from embezzlement, defalcation and misappropriation as also falsification of accounts with illicit objectives.[1]

Many facets

A fraud against a company or a corporation or a
government department may be committed in terms of its
assets, bank balance, investments, liquid cash, purchases,
wages and even stock-in-trade. The ingenuous ways in
which a fraud may be perpetrated are multiple in nature,
and will be different from incident to incident. There
will always be collusion between several employees in
case of downright misappropriation of cash and movable
assets, while for others there will also be manipulation
of books of accounts to support it.

A common method of concealing defalcation of liquid
cash is by putting through fictitious entries under
allowance disbursed to management and others. The frauds
in terms of cash may be by manoeuvring the balance in the
cash book, showing expenses against wrong vouchers,
showing assets as wrongly pledged, manipulating the loose
ledgers, jumping the petty cash books and, not infrequently, improperly inflating the valuation of assets,
particularly the stock-in-trade.[2]

Fraud may also be committed through the wage sheets,
through fictitious payments to persons who do not exist
or to wrong persons, or by showing inflated payments in
the books against deflated payments made in actual
practice.

Authorities on company law and auditing have grouped
frauds into two classes: (a) defalcation or embezzlement
involving misappropriation of money or assets, and (b)
manipulation of accounts, fraudulently, but not involving
defalcation, in order to project a financial picture of
artificial viability.[3]

Contrary to popular belief, defalcation or misappropriation of cash or assets is not easy to operate.
This requires collusion between several parties in the
organisation, and cannot be done by one single person
without the chance of early detection. If the auditor
has been able to set up in the organisation, in consulta-
tion with the management, an effective system of internal
check of books and accounts, cash and assets, chances of

such frauds will be limited.

In the opinion of the public and many authorities on accountancy and mercantile jurisprudence, the principal responsibility of auditor is to protect the organisation's assets from fraudulent manoeuvres. Prevention and detection of frauds largely overshadows all his other responsibilities. While the law has provided the auditor with some measure of protection in case a fraud has been conducted by trusted and responsible executives, there can be no gainsaying that the prevention and detection of fraud and misdemeanour continue to remain the primary responsibility of the auditor.

An antidote

Internal check is a very effective antidote against frauds. An auditor will be entirely within his rights to demand of the board of directors or the management that an effective system of internal check be instituted, and the same be under the supervision of a responsible and effective executive, preferably a chartered or incorporated accountant, who should be reasonably independent of direct executive control and surveillance.

An effective system of internal check will be able to prevent, if not forestal, possibilities of embezzlement and defalcation of cash and assets, on the one hand, and falsification of accounts, on the other. While embezzlement and defalcation are normally perpetrated as crude and downright forms of misappropriation of cash or other liquid assets, falsification or manipulation of accounts may be conducted with considerable skill and ingenuity with one or more ends in view.

There may be an attempt to project a picture of financial security for a tottering business establishment or a corporation as a sop to the shareholders, or the public, with a view to gaining their confidence. A management may also adopt these practices to show an incorrect but wider margin of profit to gain a premium on its capability and sometimes on the percentage of commission that would accrue to it.[4]

Accounts sometimes may be falsified by the directors to pay dividends in a practically losing concern. Not infrequently again, misappropriation of cash, embezzlement of funds, or defalcation of assets or investments may be the ultimate objectives. Whatever it may be, efforts are made to attain these by means of well-laid and fraudulent practices and by falsification of books and accounts, over a period of time.[5]

If the system of internal check is pervasive and effective, these can be found out in their infancy, and sometimes even before the seeds of fraud have been germinated. Nevertheless, the responsibilities of the auditor cannot be substituted by a system of internal check. It will be, therefore, in his interest to determine how far he is going to depend on the efficiency of internal check. He will indulge in a grave risk if he assumes that in view of the existence of internal check, he will hardly undertake detailed scrutiny of books and accounts.

Investigation

Investigation into frauds is one of the most important duties of an auditor, particularly when his suspicion has been excited by any loose end in the books of accounts that may have come to his notice. If any defalcation involving misappropriation of cash or stock or assets has been discovered, such investigation will have to be conducted at very great length and in considerable detail.

Where the defaulting party has had access to all the books, the auditor will be in for strenuous work. It will be necessary for him to get the whole of the postings checked, books cast, and a trial balance prepared. It will be essential for him to lead and guide the entire process of scrutiny under such circumstances. Invoices, order books, sales vouchers, contracts, payment sheets, everything will have to be given complete checkup.

The auditor will have to be on the lookout for missing returns, overwritten and fictitious credit vouchers and returns, missing pages in cash books, investment registers and such other books and returns. In respect of frauds, and particularly in the circumstances of some kind of fraud having been located, the duties of the auditor for investigation are onerous.

Sometimes a separate auditor may be appointed under the Companies Act or by moving or at the instance of the government, to specially investigate into the affairs of a company or a department or an organisation, when it is apparent that things are not at all straightforward. It may even be wise for the auditor himself to move the board of directors or the ministry for the appointment of such an investigator invoking the provisions of the Companies Act or in the interest of the taxpayer.

The liability of an auditor for frauds against the organisation has not as yet been precisely defined under the statutory enactments, except for what little is laid down or can be inferred from the company or common law or jurisprudence handed down by the courts of law. The demand on the auditor, however, is being increasingly enlarged, particularly from the point of view of the shareholders and the taxpayers.

Royal Mail case

There have been certain important law cases, under which, even though criminal liability was not exactly pinned on the auditor, the judgments contained certain specific warnings for him. There is, for instance, the

well known case of Royal Mail Steam Packet Co.[6] This
case brought the accountancy profession on its toes.
Even though the auditor was not found guilty of the
charges which purported to fix criminal liability on him,
the learned judge did caution auditors of the dangers
they would be facing if full information was not given
to the shareholders or the taxpayers of the vital affairs
of the organisation, utilisation of secret reserve for
instance.

The mouthpiece of the accountancy profession
bemoaned, "The prosecution, though unsuccessful, has
materially altered the map of the accountancy world.
Things can never again be as they were if we judge the
situation aright; auditors will not be content to run
the great risks, the existence of which has been
disclosed by the very occurrence of this case".[7]

The case was a clear pointer to an explicit change
in the norms guiding the auditor's responsibility to the
shareholders or taxpayers and his liability in the eyes
of law. The public would now look to the auditor for a
definite measure of protection. Shareholders now demand,
as do the taxpayers, if not an exact statement of the
results of current trading or turnover and sales, at
least an assurance that the results disclosed by the
accountants are not widely different from those accruing
from the ordinary trading process of the year, and are
not vitiated by fraudulent misappropriation or misdemeanour and the picture of financial viability or otherwise
has been correctly projected.[8]

It is agreed that there may be variations due to an
assortment of reasons, sometimes even connected with
company manoeuvres not quite called for, but then these
are precisely the things that the shareholders and the
taxpayers are entitled to know from the auditor. If he
fails, then the law certainly is not going to take a
lenient view of his lapses, not any more after the
definite enunciation of principles in the Royal Mail
Steam Packet Co. case.

There can be no denying that this case has opened
up new possibilities and proved to be a turning point in
the evolution of the auditor's lawful liabilities and
towards protection of shareholders and taxpayers against
possible frauds. From this time onward, the profession
could hardly close its eyes to certain definite propensities of the law, nor could it argue that the Royal
Mail case was exceptional in that the existence of current losses was not clearly brought out.

In fact, the accountancy profession has ever since
exhibited considerable resilience in not allowing such
minor issues to deflect consideration of the wider and
more general demands by the public of candour in state-
ments of accounts and nearly complete insurance against

frauds.

The precise extent of the auditor's criminal
liability, however, continues to remain, despite a
string of interesting law cases, somewhat indeterminate.
Unfortunately, management, particularly company management, gradually tends to reach newer heights in many
cases in not-quite-above-board strategies and manoeuvres.
When perpetrated in the nature of skilful manipulation
of accounts with fraudulent objectives, there is a risk
of such manoeuvres sometimes going over the head of the
watchful auditor. It is in this background that we shall
certainly expect further developments in the enunciation
of his criminal liability and his liability for misfeasance.

A watchdog or not

But is the auditor also the watchdog of the
organisation? According to Lopes L.J., he is. To the
extent he audits the affairs of the organisation, he must
be thorough, incisive and comprehensive. But then, as
was held in the case of Kingston Cotton Mills Co.,[9] the
auditor is not guilty of negligence if he accepts the
certificate of a responsible official in the absence of
suspicious circumstances.

The comments of Lopes L.J. in the course of his
judgment are very interesting... It is the duty of
an auditor to bring to bear on the work he has to perform
that skill, care and caution which a reasonably competent,
careful and cautious auditor would use. What is reasonable skill, care and caution must depend on the particular circumstances of each case. An auditor is not
bound to be a detective or, as was said, to approach
his work with suspicion or with a foregone conclusion
that there is something wrong. He is a watchdog, but
not a bloodhound.

But the phraseology, in the absence of suspicious
circumstances, is delightfully vague. In actual
practice, however, the auditor must track down circumstances to the bottom, and thereafter report to the
shareholders or the appropriate level of management
whenever there is an iota of doubt about a possible
fraud or about things not being quite straightforward.
But if there is nothing to excite his suspicion, it
will be unfair to expect the auditor to do more than his
terms of appointment would require him to do. He is
only an auditor, and therefore, cannot be called upon
to perform the functions of a CBI agent.

To refer again to the judgment delivered in the
Kingston Cotton Mills case, the auditor must not be
made liable for not tracking out ingenuous and carefully
laid schemes of fraud, when there is nothing to arouse
his suspicion, particularly when such frauds are perpetrated by tried servants of the organisation and are

undetected for years by the directors or management.

Misfeasance and the court

So far so good. This provides a measure of protection to the auditor for not over-stripping his area of functions. At the same time, one has to concede that the auditor will be held guilty of misfeasance if he fails to report to the shareholders or the taxpayers, as the case may be, when accounts are falsified, the profit and loss account does not correctly reflect the liquidity or otherwise of the organisation's assets, or when the profit and loss account or balance sheet or both have been deliberately drawn up in an improper manner to reflect an artificially bolstered viability of the company's affairs.

It should be possible for the auditor, in the very nature of his duties, to detect such practices. The auditor has a duty to examine the books of accounts, not merely for the purpose of ascertaining what they contain, but also for the purpose of satisfying himself that they show the true financial position of the company.[10]

In this context, a very well known case, re. London and General Bank,[11] threw up certain interesting conclusions. The court held that the auditor was liable for refund by way of damages, the amount of the second dividend, on the ground that he was aware of the critical position of the company's affairs, and acted negligently by not reporting the facts to the shareholders, although he reported them to the directors, and because his commission led to the declaration of the second dividend.

A full and fair balance sheet has to convey a truthful statement as to the organisation's financial and liquidity position. "It must not conceal any known cause of weakness in the financial position, or suggest anything which cannot be supported as fairly correct from a business point of view".[12] If it does, well, the auditor will have to pay for certifying such accounts as having been audited and passed.

The accountancy profession exhibited a certain measure of unrest and apprehension about rigours imposed by this judgment. The law court, however, has not relaxed, even in subsequent years, from the conclusions reached by Lindley L.J. and Rigby L.J. in the London and General Bank case. Only much later in 1936, in the case of Pendlebury's Ltd. V. Eills Green & Co.,[13] the court decided that where the directors of a private limited company are the sole shareholders, the report to the directors made by the auditors will reduce the liability of the latter to give similar information in the report to the members. But as for the company auditor of a public limited company or a government department or

corporate body is concerned, this is neither here nor
there. The liability continues unmitigated.

It would, however, have to be conceded, even by the
more radical sections of the accountancy profession, that
this liability enunciated by law need not necessarily be
resented, this being co-extensive with the basic responsibility of an auditor. After all, what is auditing?...
The object of a modern audit, although it includes the
examination of each transaction, has as its ultimate aim
the verification of the financial position disclosed by
the balance sheet and the profit and loss or revenue
account of the undertaking.

If that be so, one wonders, how the auditor can shy
away from his responsibility of ascertaining the viability of the company's financial position and liquidity
of its assets, and reporting the same to both the shareholders or the taxpayers and the directors of the
company or the department. In India particularly, this
should be of the highest importance, as ethics in management, particularly in limited companies, are not
evident everywhere.

As a profession, accountancy and auditing do yield
a fair remuneration, in comparison with other sectors of
the non-competitive professional groups. After all, when
Lopes L.J. remarked that "the duties of auditors must
not be rendered too onerous; their work is responsible
and laborious and the remuneration moderate", it was way
back in 1896. Since then the attractiveness and remuner-
ativeness of the profession has considerably grown. It
should, therefore, be appreciated that the profession
must undertake this minimum liability under the law,
under the statutes, and as enunciated in the courts of
law, as the basic principles governing auditing.
Anti-fraud law

Here we have discussed the liability of the auditor
for frauds in accounts audited by him. A mention may be
made of the responsibility of those who are found to
have perpetrated frauds, or those in charge of the
management who, in the normal discharge of their duties,
should have either been able to prevent or detect such
frauds.

The degree of responsibility would vary from
incident to incident depending upon the gravity of each
situation, the extent of the fraud and the nature of the
involvement or collusion in the perpetration of such
frauds. Fraud however is a cognizable offence and is
punishable under the Indian Penal Code[14] and a case of
proven fraud may get the perpetrator a punishment of
imprisonment for various years. It may also lead to
attachment or confiscation of property or even insolvency
proceedings,[15] against government employees or company
executives.

In a government department, a conviction in a court of law for fraud may in addition lead to removal or dismissal from service and, sometimes even forfeiture of gratuity and other dues.[16]

In the eyes of the law, collusion in the perpetration of fraud is treated nearly as rigorously as the commission of a fraud.

Liability for negligence

The auditor is liable for negligence under the common law. He has also to accept certain civil and criminal liabilities under the company law, the Fundamental Rules of Central and State governments and as adumbrated by the jurisprudence of the law court.

The written law of auditor's liability for fraud and misfeasance has not as yet been collated in one place in India. We have basically written law in India, while in the U.K. we have basically unwritten law. Unless, and until, auditing develops sufficiently as a craft in this country, it may be both premature and unwise to write down all liabilities and responsibilities of the auditor in a collated book of statute.

Certain conventions will also evolve in the law courts. Such conventions are continually developing in Britain. Thus, important cases like Irish Woollen Co. Ltd. vs. Sear, Hasluck and Co. (1904) or Arthur E.Green & Co. vs. Central Advance and Discount Corporation Ltd. (1920) threw up certain very important legal conventions for the auditor.

It has been held in these cases that an auditor is liable for any damage sustained by a company by reason of falsifications which might have been discovered by the exercise of reasonable care and skill in the performance of the audit; that the auditor is liable for any damage sustained by a concern by reason of his omission to verify the existence of assets stated in the balance sheet; that an auditor is guilty of negligence (and therefore liable for misfeasance) when he accepts a schedule of debts furnished by a responsible official, although it is apparent that other debts not included in the schedule are also irrecoverable.

Here, there may be a lot of hair-splitting on what one may call reasonable care and skill, but there should be little doubt about the intention behind the judgments and the principles that these have thrown up.[17]

Whatever little doubt the accountancy profession might have entertained about the precise and pervasive liability of the auditor in respect of frauds and misfeasance was dispelled by the judgments delivered in the Westminister Road Construction & Engineering Co.Ltd.[18] in 1932.

It was held that an auditor is guilty of misfeasance when he fails to detect the commission of liabilities

from the balance sheet in circumstances where their
commission should have been apparent. It was also held
that the auditor is guilty of misfeasance if he fails
to detect the over-valuation of work-in-progress in
circumstances where ample evidence is available for the
purpose of checking the accuracy of the figures given
to him.

Conventions and ethics

The language of the judgment leaves no ambiguity
about the extent of responsibility the court would like
the auditor to shoulder. In fact, it is now clear that
his liabilities and responsibilities are taking certain
definite shape in the eyes of law, having been determined
in a large number of important legal decisions.

The process has started in India also, and it is
expected that many more conventions, to be equally
respected by the profession and the law courts, will
duly evolve in the fields of management and auditing in
the Indian context.

A whole range of ethics will develop irrespective
of whatever might have been or might not have been laid
down in the statute books. In fact, in accountancy,
auditing, medicine and similar other professions, conventions have for a long time set out in clear and
precise terms what the statute books might not have done.
And this is, one has to admit, what it should be.

While there has been no radical change in the penal
law regarding perpetration of and collusion in fraud, the
enunciation of responsibility and liability of a government employee have lately given a new direction to the
extent of responsibility for frauds in a government
department or corporate body.

Removal and dismissal from service may really be
only the first step in punitive action that the state
may elect to initiate, followed by attachment and forfeiture of gratuity, funds and dues, and in many cases,
prosecution in law courts. Fraud and misfeasance have
become very slippery and dangerous alleys to tread upon.
If the recent trend continues, greater rigour in the
penal enactments is also indicated.

As in case of black market or black money deals or
smuggling, fraud and misfeasance are also committed by
distorted or degenerate elements in the employ of government departments or companies, or by likeminded persons
aiding and abetting with them, or both. Red eyes of the
law and the efficacy of the enforcement machinery are
two deterrents. Another equally important preventive
deterrent is the effectiveness of internal check and
auditing, and to that end, the liability and responsibility shouldered by the auditors.

NOTES
1. Indian Companies Act, amended to-date.
2. S.K. Ray - Company Frauds and Jurisprudence;
Economic Times, Bombay, January 26, 1975.
3. Spicer & Peglar - Practical Auditing; Tenth
Edition (1951); Sir Issac Pitman & Sons Ltd., London.
4. S.K. Ray - Company Frauds, Auditor's Liability &
Jurisprudence; Business Standard, Calcutta, April 7,1975.
5. Ibid.
6. Rex V. Kylsant and Morland, 1931 (Accountant,
1931 L.R., P.109 onwards). This case came to be known
as the Royal Mail case, as the suit was brought against
the auditors of Royal Mail Steam Packet Co.,Ltd.
7. The Accountant, London, 1931.
8. S.K. Ray - Jurisprudence of Auditing; Eastern
Economist, New Delhi, July 12, 1968.
9. Re. Kingston Cotton Mills Co. Ltd. (No.2),1896.
10. Ranking, Peglar and Spicer - The Rights and
Duties of Liquidators, Trustees and Receivers; 21st
Edition; Sir Isaac Pitman & Sons Ltd., London.
11. Re. London and General Bank (No.2) (1895 2 CH 673).
12. Ibid.
13. Re. Pendlebury's Ltd. V. Eills Green & Co.(1936,
80 Acct. L.R. 39).
14. Sections 246, 247, 420 to 424 of the Indian
Penal Code, 45 of 1860.
15. (i) Insolvency Act; Act V of 1920. (ii) Indian
Trusts Act, VI of 1882. (iii) Disciplinary Action &
Appeal Rules and Fundamental Rules for Central & State
Government Establishments in India.
16. Ibid.
17. S.K. Ray - Frauds and Jurisprudence; Business
Standard, Calcutta; April 8, 1975.
18. Re. The Westminister Road Construction &
Engineering Co. Ltd., 1932, (Acctt. February 1932,
P.203-204).

9

Corruption
in Public Life

It would be presumptive to think that corruption is
exclusive to developing economies. While the state of
economic development has much to do with the standard of
living, corruption in public life is a direct corollary
to national character.[1] The decadence in public life in
ancient Rome and Egypt do bear testimony to this conclusion. In many advanced countries today there are
corrupt influences in trade and industry, but their
effects on the national economy do not impose such an
overwhelming burden as in some of the developing countries.

The effect of corruption is also governed by what
Taussig enunciated as the principle of <u>what the traffic
will bear</u>. It is said that in the national economy of
a number of developed countries there is high-money
politicking. The influence of corruption in national
elections exploded in the U.S.A. into limelight after
<u>the Watergate affair</u>. In the formation of cartels and
other forms of monopoly groups, corruption of a bizarre
character are frequently reported in the national press,
and sometimes even extensive underhand linkages with
governmental and political influences do come to light.

But, for the purpose of the present study, we are
concerned with the effects of corruption on the national
economy: the way it affects the price level and standard
of living. While high-money manoeuvres as in the U.S.A.
are involved in the formation of cartels and other
monopoly-groups, these have led to intense competition
between the monopoly-groups and consequently to higher
productivity and expansion of international trade. The
final result not infrequently has been a widening market
for the national industries and more favourable balance
of payments, resulting in an increase in the level of
prosperity. Such corruption by itself did not by and
large lead to a hijacking of the price spiral or a
lowering in the standard of living of the people.

115

116

Tentacles

This is not so in case of a number of developing
economies. Corruption in such countries is comparable
to the manoeuvres of a deep-sea octopus. It has a multitude of tentacles. It has pervaded not only in the
government offices, but also in extensive measure into
private industries. It is perpetrated by one common
man against another. It is indulged in by the petty
corporation official against the man in the street and
even against another petty government official.

The ways of corruption are not always ingenuous,
and sometimes they are not even looked down upon as a
social evil. The influence of corruption are so deep-
seated that often it is not even decried or protested
against. Payments made under corruptions are often
considered regular payments required to be made for a
service rendered or a product supplied, ranging from
mamul to party funds.[2]

It is common knowledge that in a district office,
a person often does not even hesitate to give a fixed
amount for the renewal of an arms license, in a municipal
office for fixed amounts payable for a new water connection, or in a rationing office for issue of a ration
card. In government offices staff in office dealing with
the payments of overtime or running allowance bills etc.
of their own colleagues charge a fixed amount of mamul
without which the bills get stuck for several real or
discovered shortcomings.[3]

Sometimes even this is not good enough. Bargains
for lumpsum payments are required to be settled with the
babus before a bill for arrear is processed, or even
before an advance taken from the provident fund for one's
daughter's marriage is billed for payment.

A noted observer said at the end of Asia's colonial
period, "In nearly all Asian countries there has always
been a tradition of corruption. Officials were not well-
paid and had to make ends meet. The well-timed bribe
which was often almost a conventional fee, was the
emollient which made the wheels of administration turn
most efficiently".[4]

The malaise

Any amount of debate can be waged about the ways of
corruption being as rampant in the west at different
stages of history as in the east; but the fact remains
that in the developing countries corruption in public
life and its forces being active in the economy have an
age-old tradition, and today, this has seeped into the
cores of the economic firmament.

In everyday parlance, corruption stands for some
form of moral delinquency. The Webster's Dictionary
tells us that it signifies perversion of anything from
an original state of purity.

The public opinion on morality has not been
uniform over the ages; the standards have changed from
one century to another, or from the turn of a century to
another. But one thing is for sure, that the standard of
morality in public life does reflect the socio-economic
situation at any particular point of time.

A student of British political history knows that
there was a time in England when Servants of the Crown
made personal gains out of the public purse.[5] Similarly,
a student of Indian history knows about the huge amounts
of public money Clive or Hastings had plundered at the
cost of the East India Company they represented, and
that their practices have not come to an end even today,
and that, if at all, the position has only worsened.

A graph of corruption, drawn over a substantial
period of time, for a representative economy, may look
something like that of prices, rocketing up at times
with manifest breakdown of moral standards, and at times
resting on a plateau, when the economy is bouyant and
there is prosperity around.

One should not be removed from the basic truth that
the incidence of corruption is perhaps inversely propor-
tional to excellence of public administration and
integrity of national character together with the state
of productivity of the economy and the extent of the net
national product.

India

Coming to India, one can attempt to trace out the
evolution of corruption in Indian public life right from
the days of Kautilya. In the days of Arthashastra
(roughly the beginning of third century B.C.), though
there were occasional instances of corruption in ancient
judiciary, the standards set for the judiciary and the
magistracy were very high.

Kautilya's Arthashastra in fact prescribed that the
honesty of the judiciary should be periodically tested
by agents provocateurs. Says Kautilya, "Just as it is
impossible not to taste honey or the poison that finds
itself at the tip of the tongue, so it is impossible for
a government servant not to eat up, at least a bit, of
the King's revenue. Just as a fish moving under water
cannot possibly be found out either as drinking or not
drinking water, government servants employed as state
functionaries cannot be found out (while) taking money
(for themselves)".[6]

Kautilya holds that case of embezzlement or no
embezzlement can be ascertained through spies alone -
the precursors of modern vigilance and intelligence
officers.

Incidentally, Vishnu Smriti prescribed banishment
and forfeiture of property for a judge found guilty of
corruption or injustice, this having been the most

severe penalty for a <u>brahman</u> under the sacred laws. That corruption was not the mainstay of Indian public life has been illustrated in ample measure in the writings of the Greek traveller-statesman Megasthenes.

Ashoka's <u>dharmic</u> state, a state governed by the precepts of religion, following closely on the heels of Kautilya's times, must have had a minimum of corruption, for the Emperor declared in one of his edicts: "For the welfare of all folk is what I must work for", and to this end he commended that for despatch of business, his officials will report to him at all times and hours, "whether I am dining, or in the ladies' apartments, in my bed-room, or in my closet, in my carriage, or in the palace gardens".[7]

When the emperor himself meant to enforce such expedition in official business, it was but natural that the message went home to his officials all along the line, and people did not have to use emollient to get their job done. In the modern state, it is not infrequently that while, on the one hand, the virtues of expedition are extolled, the actual concepts practised are expediency and misfeasance.

Corruption was, however, rampant in the Pathan and Mughal periods, even in the heyday of the glory of the 16th century A.D. Sir Thomas Roe wrote: "The people live as fishes do in the sea, the great ones eat up the little; the farmer robs the peasant, the gentleman robs the farmer, the greater robs the lesser, and the king robs all".[8]

Francisco Pelsart, Chief of the Dutch Factory at Agra, wrote way back in 1629, "The second scourge is the oppression of Governor, nobles, Diwan, Kotwal, Bakshi, and other imperial officers. If one of these wants a workman, the man is not asked if he is willing to come, but is seized in his house or in the street, well beaten if he should dare to raise any objection, and in the evening paid half his wages, or perhaps nothing at all. This was worse than corruption, for the sufferer sacrificed money and got nothing in return except a few blows".

In the early days of East India Company's rule, now it is a part of history, many civil and military officials coming to India had shaken the pagoda-tree and returned home with ill-gotten riches. <u>Shaking the pagoda-tree</u> was a grand name for operations which involved corruption, theft and extortion.

British rule thereafter tried to reduce corruption at higher echelons by keeping them free from temptation by paying them adequately.

The Islington Commission laid down the principles of public salaries. The Commission recognised the existence of extensive corruption in public life, and recommended that "the only safe criterion is that

Government should pay so much only to their employees as
is necessary to obtain recruits of the right stamp and
to maintain them in such a degree of comfort and dignity
as will shield them from temptation". How far, however,
was this policy a success or even sincere was another
matter altogether.

It has however been said that the laissez faire
policy of the government of the day was responsible for
reducing the incidence of network corruption. The
government believed in collective land revenue, maintaining law and order and rendering such public service
as the artificially limited budgets of those days
permitted. The areas of control by the government over
the economy, and the resultant scope for corruption and
misfeasance, was perhaps comparatively less extensive.

This, however, has been a rather one-sided interpretation of the situation. During the British period,
the government was much more interested in sustaining a
colonial economy with imperial preferences than in
fostering grooves of corruption for its subjects. What
would today be known as corruption was in fact extortion
then, while imperial privilege was another name for
misfeasance.

It has also to be appreciated that the expectation
of fair play under a foreign rule was much lesser, and,
therefore, the moral standards to judge corruption and
misfeasance in public life were also altogether
different.

During the second world war, and in the years that
followed, it has been felt that corruption in India as
in many other countries has unfortunately escalated in
hundred myriad ways. Because of its very nature, we
have no systematic information of the shape and size of
the new monster of corruption, but by all accounts
these are rather formidable.

Reports do, however, come in the Indian press,
every year, of the number of officials of various ranks
arrested, prosecuted, convicted and jailed by the
central and state governments. Even though the figures
published are themselves substantial, in absolute number,
they obviously reflect only a small fraction of the
incidents of corruption by public officials, and, therefore, their corrective effect is no more than of the
stone thrown in a flowing river in an effort to bridge
the same.

Even so, the list of officers proceeded against is
very impressive. Secretaries to government, commissio-
ners, heads of departments, chief engineers, superintend-
ing engineers, and others of similar ranks, not to
speak of lesser officials, do adorn the roll of honour.

Corruption, in the last few decades, has emerged
more or less as a national malady, in a number of

developing economies, serious enough to be taken notice of and subjected to investigations by committees appointed by the governments. In India, the Santhanam Committee on Public Administration and the Kripalani Committee on Railways, were two such committees that went into a scrutiny of the malaise.

The reports of the Santhanam and Kripalani Committees in India, however, more or less depicted the <u>trends</u> of corruption prevalent in the country, particularly in government offices, their conclusions based not only on the basis of replies to questionnaires issued but also on a critical analysis of <u>trends</u>.[9]

Developing countries

In a number of developing economies of the world, which during the last few decades have been able to dismantle foreign rule, a disturbing trend has been identified by social scientists. In order to gain control over bureaucracy, many representatives of the people, in and out of the political parties, in and outside power, people sometimes with doubtful virtues and competence, largely sheltering under the protection of politics "took to browbeating the officials, scared them with the exercise of their political power and indulged in a game of witch-hunt for the so-called corrupt unobliging elements in the public services".

This has been called from <u>Maccarthyism</u> in U.S.A. to anti-Islam in Uganda. In many Asian countries, it has not been christened with any such aphorism, but officers and officials not falling in line have been treated as anti-establishment and anti-people. The bureaucracy in these countries frequently caved in, to save its skin, and became subservient to the predatory power of the politician. Those who did not, frequently went through a maze of change of posts and transfers - the most effective weapon to bring up the <u>unwilling</u> official.

It was to the advantage of the corrupt elements in public life in some of these developing economies to weaken the administration. Behind the facade of the friends and representatives of the people, political pressure-groups had formed in the corridors of government offices. The twists of degenerate politics have been responsible for introducing the virus of corruption into the body politic of such countries.

The importance of this phenomenon at a cross-road of world history is not fully appreciated. Most of these countries had a well-knit and organised administration with directly recruited cadres of officers with zeal, ambition, loyalty and foresight. The potentials were really immense for these cadres forging to provide the independent administration a clean and competent administration.

The opportunity, however, was largely lost at that stage in view of the politicians browbeating and corrupting them at every stage, letting loose in these countries a network of influences and pressures, and very frequently knocking the honest administrator out as indiscreet and obstructive, and, what is the final irony, sitting in judgment over the same officials once the worse is done, or the tide changes. A competent and honest administrator frequently found himself on a difficult terrain against the manoeuvres of pressure politics.

An Indian survey

The Indian Institute of Public Opinion at New Delhi conducted a worthwhile survey in 1972 about the extent of corruption in the Indian economy. This was a metropolitan survey of the peoples' assessment on corruption and the resultant crisis of public confidence in the Indian public life. This assessment was made on the basis of 500 interviews. The results of the survey were made public through a special Commentary on Indian Economic Conditions issued by the Institute.

The summary of the results of the survey does provide interesting material in the context of corruption in Indian public life. How do the people at large assess the extent and impact of the new corruption ? The relatively small metropolitan (500 interviews) survey aimed to find a quantitative answer to this question.

We cannot credit the results of the survey conducted by the Indian Institute of Public Opinion with accuracy. The results, however, are indicative of the general trend of affairs. The major findings of the Survey have been summarised in the subsequent paragraphs.

1. Seven in ten persons interviewed in the course of the survey were of the opinion that during the course of a decade our moral standards in public life have taken a downhill plunge. This dismal view was shared by people from all walks of life, regardless of their economic and educational status, in all the four cities.

2. A far more disturbing picture emerged when the question was posed in more specific terms. It is one of crisis of confidence in the character of the political elite. Three in four persons were of the view that such persons suffer from a serious credibility-gap on this score.

3. Nor were Big Business and retail traders spared. But, the image of senior and middle level civil servants is not by and large tarnished. But the fact that many persons in politics come under heavier fire brings into sharp focus the damage done to public morale, because of the disastrous and simmering influence of politicians on the body politic.

4. That this crisis of confidence runs deep is seen in the responses to follow-up questions. If the conclusions reached in this survey by the Institute of Public Opinion is any guide, the people were finding bureaucracy unresponsive and frequently misfeasant, particularly at the grass-root levels.

5. The higher and middle levels of civil servants have been thwarted over the years in their confrontation with corrupt ways by political brow-beating and pressure strategies. In this, they have been further thwarted by econo-political subversions, often waged by misguided trade unionism. No wonder, many of them started blinking their eyes and circumventing the ways of controversy.

6. No wonder that, the survey concludes, the people find themselves on the threshold of frustration. And in this frustration lies the roots of popular resignation. There is evidence in this survey that the popular mood on corruption is veering towards apathy. One in four persons admitted they had come to accept the phenomenal increase in corruption as a fact of life and that they just did not care any more. A large majority (65 percent) however expressed concern. But it may only be a question of time before chunks of people from this sixty-five percent also start getting disillusioned, and give up their daily whimper or wail of protest.

7. Popular frustration is reflected even more graphically in the response to a set of state-ments offered to respondents with a view to bringing out the range of their feelings and views on the issue. It was the corruption at the political level that was the worst malady, as this bred further corruption down the ladder.

8. A large proportion (86 percent) thought corrup-tion could be controlled if exemplary punishment was meted out to the guilty. The difficulty to this, in the background of what has been stated already, is multi-pronged. First, it may be like poking a stick in a beehive. Second is the law of the land which builds up a legal process based on the laws of evidence. Third and final is the fact that petty corruption thrives because of the feverish hikes in the price spiral and the inequity in distribution which were the responsibilities of the state to prevent after independence.

9. Once the people are convinced that corruption has become too pervasive to be controlled by

government or popular protest, they are bound to _resign_ themselves to the situation, the Survey concludes. "When vice is regarded highly rewarding and can be indulged in with impunity, virtue tends to lose its relevance in general ethical standards. The process of permissiveness then gathers momentum and most persons not only turn a blind eye to what was hitherto regarded ethically reprehensible but also start waiting for their chance".

10. The Survey wonders if this is not already happening in Indian society today. Not that the people at large have become permissive; they simply _look askance_ at this sorry spectacle. While living standards of the common man have hardly risen, there has emerged a _nouveau riche_ upper class, with some of the cases being examples of 'rags to riches'... There is an element of glamour attached to the new rich, and this acts continuously to sap through the moral resistance to tread the correct path for the ambitious left-outs. As there is a limit to the expansion of the _nouveau riche_ in a sluggishly expanding economy, this ambitious segment of the left-outs would blink on virtue; certainly not when it has become so unrewarding.

Conclusions

Thus the appetite for corruption will whet by what it feeds upon; not only in those who are corrupt but also in those "to whom the spectacle of the wicked flourishing like the green banyan tree breeds revolt and anger".

As Tocqueville said, "what is to be feared is not so much the immorality of the great as the fact what immorality may lead to greatness. An odious connection is thus formed between the ideas of turpitude and power, unworthiness and success, utility and dishonour".

It is difficult, as was said in the beginning, to entirely agree with the conclusions reached by the Survey conducted by the Institute of Public Opinion in India. For one thing, the survey was too limited in scope to be representative, and for another, it is felt that both the questionnaire as also the responses were themselves tainted by cynicism and hearsay.

But the survey certainly indicated a _trend_, and that by itself was bad enough. We might debate about the _degrees_ of corruption in public life, in India and a number of other developing countries, but there can be no more any controversy that the malaise is extensive _and_ deep-seated and would require nothing short of a major remedial surgery in the public life of such countries.

In other words, where do we go from here ? Bemoaning the degeneration of the national character alone will not do. Nor is a crusade for a sudden regeneration of the national character likely to deliver results. Moral crusades tend to reach an early satiation point in the receptivity of the target groups. What is more, they more often than not attract humbugs, faddists and plain charlatans. Even when, in the rare event, such crusades deliver the goods, it is in the longer haul.

What is to be done, in the meantime ? Here, there is need for a very difficult piece of heart-searching.

The problem is more political than ethical, for it has acquired far-reaching political implications. Naturally, therefore, it calls for a political solution. And it has to be tackled at the highest political levels. Whatever party may be in power in each of these countries, for its own long-term survival, if not for the people's sake, will have to weed out the corrupt from its ranks regardless of their status, before they go about others![10]

Righteous condemnation of corrupt officials alone will not do. Many political heads will have to roll before popular faith is restored in the integrity of politicians. Once this is done, it will have salutary effect on officials down the ladder. Once this happens, and in the correct way, and not as a convenient witch-hunt for the political opponent, other things for cleansing the slate will automatically follow suit.

True, due process of law in a democracy may not help in bringing the guilty to book for want of legally tenable proof. But once the objective has been decided, the inadequacies in the law of the land can be probed by a committee of juristic and economic experts, and effective legislations can be enacted to tackle corrupt and misfeasant officials and others under the due process of law.

In the field of trade, industry and commerce, government will have to empower itself with adequate statutory powers and come down with heavy hand over large-scale corruption, misfeasance and turpitude of social standards affecting life of the people and growth of the economy.

In order to achieve this, the government and the political party in power, of whatever shade it may be, and whatever the country may be, will have to **first** establish its own credibility about honesty and integrity with the people. **Rest** will not be difficult.

The problem of petty corruption,[11] of course, will remain. But then a nation can always survive petty corruption. It is the big corruption that eats away the vitals of its socio-economic set-up. It is the corruption at high decision-making levels and big business involving black money that deprives a nation of

significant sums needed for development and the will to
act with single purpose directed to the national good.

In the long run, therefore, <u>the sharks have to be</u>
fettered, and in this the politician and the government,
as the leaders of the people, have to take the lead.
There is no other way out. And this is true for India
as also for any other country in the world, particularly
those who have thrown off foreign domination and are
presently engaged in building up a developing economy.[12]

NOTES

1. Telleyrand is credited with the observation
that corruption is a matter of <u>period</u>.

2. Statement made by T.A. Pai, a former Indian
Minister for Railways, and later, Industries, during
April 1977. He was also a Vice-Chancellor of Delhi
University.

3. Ramesh Thapar - <u>Bureaucratic Collapse</u>; The
Statesman, New Delhi; August 24, 1980.

4. "It is not seemly nor of good report that thieves
at home must hang, but he that puts into his overgorged
purse, the wealth of Indian provinces, escapes".

5. <u>Indian History - British Period</u>; Bharatiya Vidya
Bhavan, New Delhi.

6. R. Shamasastry - <u>Kautilya's Arthashastra</u>; fifth
edition; Raghuveer Press, Mysore, 1956.

7. R.C. Mazumdar - <u>Ancient India</u>; <u>The Reign of
Dharmashoka</u>.

8. <u>Indian History: British Period</u>; Bharatiya Vidya
Bhavan, New Delhi.

9. The reports of the Santhanam and Kripalani
Committees on corruption remain, till today, the exclusive researches on corruption in India's body politic.
Lately, Wanchoo Committee's Report focussed attention
on economic corruption and black money.

10. Ramesh Thapar - <u>Bureaucratic Collapse</u>; The
Statesman, New Delhi; August 24, 1980.

11. K.N. Subramanian, in a research paper published
in Economic Times, Bombay in September 1973, collated
an anthology of petty and not-so-petty corruption in
the Indian socio-political life.

12. S.K. Ray - <u>Corruption and the Economy</u>;Business
Standard, Calcutta, January 17 & 18, 1978.

S.K. Ray - <u>Shaking the Pagoda Tree</u>; Economic
Times, Bombay, May 21, 1978.

S.K. Ray - <u>Corruption in Public Life</u>; The Hindu,
Madras, June 25, 1979.

10

Strategy
for a Combat

The damages caused by the black market slowly become highly pestering, inasmuch as a successful black-marketeer, or a group of them, often tends to hold a grip on the market, thereby imparting to the black market some sort of a perpetuity. Necessity therefore arises for effectively crushing this market.

While economists are loud against the black market, and the black money that it fosters, there is little unanimity of views as to the strategy for its liquidation. There are some economists who hold that the diffusion of a moral sense of justice is an appropriate remedy.[1]

Clay in his <u>Economics for the General Reader</u> wrote about social prerogative and individual prerogative amongst businessmen. He observed that by moral persuasion businessmen should be made to socialize their business endeavours. Walker, Dimcock, Bye and Hewett and a number of other economists supported him. They advised businessmen and entrepreneurs that "it is to society's interest that they should reflect on and realise the social effects of their private actions".
<u>A change of mind</u>

This lobby of economists pinned their faith on a possible change of mind. They are more or less the followers of the classical school of economists, led by Kahn and Marshall, and a few of the neo-classicals like Pigou and Cole. They have always considered economics as a study of philosophy in the economic field (philosophy of political economy, as they called it), and were inclined to believe, pinning their faith on the basic goodness of the human mind, that the erring businessmen and entrepreneurs could always be persuaded to give up their anti-social pursuits, and that way black business could be won over without bloodshed.

In the actual work-a-day life, however, it has been a recurrent experience that the principle of moral persuasion has been, as far as it goes, nothing more

than an eulogy. And despite this social approach to
business, industrial or business enterprise has frequently manifested itself in unsocial, private and utterly
individualistic tendencies.

Thus we have experienced how legitimate speculation
has been reduced to illegitimate gambling, stock of
foodgrains has been hoarded in order to create artificial
scarcity, and prices have been pushed up by sterilising
the age-old economic laws. At the same time, by artificial manipulation of consumption-propensity and thereby
affecting the level of demand, the spiral potential of
prices has been tapped by the black-market operators to
accumulate inflated profits.

One has to appreciate that there is hardly any use
in preaching the gospel to a bunch of anti-social
businessmen. It is in recognition of this fact of life
that government control started being given a serious
thought as an antidote to erring business endeavours by
economists like Lerner and Stein.

Government control

Government control over economic activities in
expanding waves is an essential characteristic of the
work-a-day life in the free economies of the world. It
is not that this has come about only in any single country, or in selected economic sectors like production or
distribution. "The movement today is not only persistent
but also extensive, so much so that it is no more
possible to attribute it to the belief of only a few
cloistered theorists or reformers". It is today a
distinct infrastructure of economy in India as in any
other democratic country.

In a totalitarian economy, there is hardly anything
outside the sphere of government control, and with
complete or near-complete regimentation of economic
activity, chances of black business or smuggling or tax
evasion and generation of black money become lean in view
of the ruthless tightening of screws the government is
likely to apply. In fact, general taxation and loans
hardly provide 10 percent of revenues in USSR.[2]

But the situation is different in free-market
economies, where democratic governments of varying shades
are in position. In such economies, private economic
enterprise and socio-economic decisions of the individuals still hold the centre of the stage. What is
important is that in almost all such economies there has
been an increasing recognition and acceptance of the
state functioning as a catalytic agent for economic
development. For such countries, "government regulation
is a silent partner in all economic activity and an
active partner in most economic activity".

Economic regulation

A whole range of complicated problems gets into

focus while considering economic regulation as a strategy
for economic development... Thus, what are equitable
distribution arrangements? How can black marketing be
liquidated, tax-evasion prevented, profiteering curbed,
black money unearthed and smuggling halted? Will
demonetisation help? Should devaluation be on the card?

While these questions require to be answered at one
level of decision-making, at another level are the more
poignant issues relating to the weighing of balances
amidst, and coordinating various public policies impinging
on, the sectoral and national economy.

Extension of government controls of different sorts
and in different areas, particularly in such complicated
fields as the contra-distinct pulls of international
trade, forces of a parallel economy unleashed by black
market and black money, high-finance econo-political
manoeuvres of smuggling and economic espionage, create
multitudinal problems.

The spate of issues relating to the decision-making
process do not terminate here. Towards the apex of the
process rest such problems, the solution to which will
have profound import on economic life. There are such
questions as these... Is economic freedom to be equated
with economic license? If not, at what stage is the
government required to step in and cry a halt? In a
fight against the forces of a parallel economy, "can
expanding government control of economic life continue
its past inexorable progress, while at the same time
preserving the fundamental economic and political
freedom?"[3]

The question that crops up would be whether increasing state control "would lead towards a collectivist
economy, may be not so much by choice, as by the immuta-
bility of an expansionary chain reaction of government
control".[4]

The day, when free enterprise and government planning
could be considered as antipodal economic concepts has
long since gone past. "It is the problem of devising
for this day and age a relationship between public and
private interests which will achieve the fundamental
goals that society collectively sets for its social and
economic system".[5]

Choice between the extremes

In 1846, Mecaulay observed, "There is no more
important problem than to ascertain the just mean
between these two most pernicious extremes, to draw
correctly the line which divides those cases in which
it is the duty of the state to interfere from those
cases in which it is the duty of the state to abstain
from interference". A few years later John Stuart Mill
observed, "One of the most disputed questions at this
particular time, relates to the proper limits of the

functions and agency of governments..." These words can be used in today's context of economic policy without any loss of significance.

There can be no two opinions that in a combat against the evils of black market and black money, tax evasion and smuggling, the principal <u>activist role</u> will rest with the government. This does not mean, on the one hand, that economic freedom needs to be equated with economic license, and on the other, that government restraints, surveillance and enforcement have to lead to a collectivist or totalitarian economy.

We cannot but, therefore, emphasise the need for an integrated approach. As was versified by John G. Saxe from a story of <u>the Panchatantra</u>, the Indian classic fable:

And so these men of Indostan
Disputed loud and long,
Each in their own opinion
Exceeding stiff and strong,
Though each was partly in the right
And all were in the wrong.[6]

It should be possible for India to maintain an individual enterprise system, benefit from the demonstrable advantages of individual initiative in improving social and economic welfare, while at the same time restraining the excess of individualism and liquidating black markets, black money and smuggling. It should be possible to construct a happy solution to the problem of resolving powerful government with responsible government.[7]

Must India embrace regimentation to solve today's socio-economic ailments, like the black market and smuggling thriving on black money, and in the process, abandon the basic concepts of individual freedom?...The indomitable Prime Minister of India,[8] with the usual courage of her convictions, has asserted that it should be possible for the country to liquidate the evil forces of corruption and economic offences, and attain optimum economic development, within the framework of democracy.

Neither full economic license nor economic regimentation will be necessary in the struggle against black market and other allied pursuits; well-conceived governmental measures, planned and legislated with economic and legal expertise and executed with sincerity and adroitness, will certainly achieve the desired objectives.

Having thus established the role of government measures in the struggle against black market and black money, tax-evasion and smuggling, we may now proceed to examine the effectiveness of the different measures already introduced in Indian and other economic systems

of the world at different points of time since the second
world war, and in the process isolate and develop the
measures that should be put on the cards in India or in
a number of other countries of the world suffering from
similar socio-economic ailments.

Shortages and price control

Referring back to our analysis in chapter 2, one
essential attribute of market behaviour in a thriving
black market will be shortages, which may reflect either
the actual situation of supply or one of artificial
manipulation. Whatever it may be, the supply curve will
be such in relation to the demand curve that a contracted
supply will try to catch up with a stagnant or increasing
demand.[9]

The difference between scarcity and shortage is best
illustrated by the function of prices in a free market
vitiated by black market conditions.[10] In an unregulated
market, as a commodity becomes scarce, prices immediately
rise to the point where purchasers accommodate themselves
to the smaller amounts forthcoming. The commodity does
not altogether disappear from the market; it is available
to those who can afford the black market price on the
sly. If, however, government enforces a ceiling on prices below the equilibrium level that would obtain in an
unrestrained black market, stocks would disappear from
the open market altogether.[11]

The first principle is, therefore, that any attempt
to fix a price by authority, without control of either
production or consumption, is prone to failure unless,
of course, the price fixed happens to be the price which
would have been established in the black market.

When the state passes a law legislating price-
ceilings or prohibiting transactions in which the price
is different from the one specified by such law, it is
a case of price-fixation or, in some case, price-regula-
tion. This has been done in India times without number
for essential commodities like rice, wheat, sugar, cement,
iron and steel and hydrogenated cooking oil. It has
however been the experience that in most cases, and for
most of the commodities, either the law has been evaded
or the transaction ceased to take place(black marketing
in the first instance and hoarding in the second), or
the government has been obliged 'to interfere drastically
with the production or distribution or even consumption
of the commodity'.

This is abundantly illustrated by the history of
price fixing, for instance during the second world war,
in the Indian sub-continent.[12] The Indian government
at first essayed to stop the rising price of major foodgrains by firmans or ordinances. What happened? In
most cases the commodities disappeared from the market
altogether, giving over the reins to a thriving black

market.

    If the price which the government fixed "was below
that at which the most efficient producer or trader found
that it paid to produce or buy and sell", then there was
simply very little production or transaction above board.
Alternatively, for some time at least, there was no further sale in the open market, the entire commodity being
cornered and then hoarded, for later release on black
market counters.[13]

Consumers' resistance movement

    There have been certain price resistance movements
in India. These have been, however, almost completely
confined to the metropolitan areas, particularly Bombay,
Delhi and Calcutta. Their effectiveness, however, has
been next to nothing, and in effect these have been little
beyond whimpers of protest. There are some price resistance movements by housewives still alive in Bombay and
Delhi, but these also have recorded no worthwhile result.

    In countries like the U.S.A., however, price-
resistance movements have had greater impact on the
price-situation or on the government policy relating to
demand, supply and prices of essential consumables. The
principal reason behind the relative success of the
movement in U.S.A. has been its extensive organisation,
adequately backed by finance and publicity.

    These movements have had little or no success in
India, because these have been no more than occasional
spot-protests, and never in the nature of a mass movement
of resistance. The participation has also been limited
and even when there was participation of housewives there
was no change whatsoever in their impact, except possibly
for a measure of embarrassment caused to the local administration.

    Such a movement can have a future in India only if
it can be transmuted to a mass movement, not confined to
urban areas alone, when it is not organised only in the
nature of protests against the government, and when it is
in the shape of a real resistance movement by the people.
Thus, suppose the retail price of sugar go beyond a
particular level as a result of the back-lash of black
marketing, people should agree to go without sugar for a
week, a fortnight, or a month, until the prices come down,
and a clearance is given by the resistance committee to
buy sugar.

    At the moment, there does not appear to be much of
an organisation or following in evidence for such a movement. The manoeuvres of the black market operators and
the wide disparity in income distribution in the country
are the two major hurdles in the way of development of
such an effective resistance movement.

Rationing

    Amongst the different methods deployed by the

government for an equitable sponsored distribution system by a control over purchases, rationing has been the most widely used and effective method. The government issues ration cards or coupons entitling every individual to a fixed quantity. If rationing is to be successful, the total ration in any period must be about equal to the quantity coming in the market for sale. Purchases are then restricted not by the price, but by the total quantity available.[14]

To cope with an emergency - situation of scarcity, such as those created by a crop failure or war or by the rampage of floods or droughts, rationing with price control are effective socio-economic measures, compared to a method of free play of prices by interaction of demand and supply. In the latter case the rich, particularly the new rich, may bid the prices of basic necessities beyond the reach of the common man or the middle class, and what is worse, may thereupon channelise the supply to the black market hoards for further profiteering.

One has to reckon that enforcement of rationing bristles with difficulties of its own. Any effort by government to enforce need-based allocation of commodities is liable to be crude. "Equal distribution is not equitable if needs are different". Consequently rationing can be fairly effective when needs are approximately equal, such as sugar and rice; when extended to more complex commodities such as petrol or clothing, the system gradually becomes more and more complicated, with different rations for different classes of people. The wider the field of rationing, the more difficult it is to apportion successfully.[15]

An almost inevitable consequence of price control and rationing is the development of the black market, an illegal market in which transactions take place above the legal price. The mechanism of the black market as a result of price control and rationing has been amply illustrated in our market investigations in chapter 2 earlier in this thesis.[16]

How can price-control, price-stabilisation and rationing be made to work smoothly, without these themselves giving rise to a proliferated black market ?... The answer is very simple, and the sooner it is faced the better. It should be possible for the state to enforce rationing and price regulation, and for this purpose it should not only be armed with highly deterrent powers for seizure, detention and legal penalties, but should also be in a position and willing to enforce them.

The blackmarketeers are after all renegades from the law, and they only understand the red eyes of the law and ruthless tightening of the screws by the government. No other method would work with them.

Network problems

Too intricate a texture of controls and permits
however generate corruption, and thereafter black market
and tax evasion. As was said by the DTEC, controls and
rationing on the one hand, and black money on the other,
contribute a vicious circle. Even as controls generate
black market, black market generates black money and tax
evasion. Controlled goods carry a premium and the
premium is always given and demanded in cash to escape
detection .[17]

Not only goods but certain entitlements and rights
in the form of licenses and permits, import licenses for
instance, command a premium on the sly. Rent controls
have given rise to the infamous 'pugree system'. After
the second world war, permits for ration shops used to
fetch huge amounts of misfeasance-premium in greater
Calcutta, and naturally, therefore, ration shops themselves became both hoards and counters of the black market.

The clandestine deals and undisclosed investments
arising from black money have caused a serious problem
of tax evasion which increases in geometric progression,
as "black money generates more black money and evasion
breeds further evasion".[18]

In a developing economy, which is frequently ravaged
by droughts, crop failures, shortage of foreign exchange
and difficulties in investment, controls and permits are
necessary. These also become necessary in view of a
raging black market growing in the economy. Wanchoo
Committee therefore recommended a review of all existing
controls and permits.

The prevalent arguments[19] which seek a minimisation
of controls and licenses can be summarised as under:

1. Over the years some controls outlive their
   utility; others become difficult to administer;
   while the ills they seem to cure persist, there
   is the added problem of black money and tax
   evasion; some become redundant in that they
   affect or benefit only a small section of the
   community, which tends to acquire a vested
   interest in their continuance.
2. Some controls even inhibit or hamper production,
   thereby perpetuating shortages. Still others
   might be so open to abuse that it is not worthwhile having them at all.
3. In some cases, the economic situation might have
   so changed that rethinking is necessary on the
   utility of retaining such controls. There has
   in fact been some rethinking from time to time
   in this regard, as is evidenced by control,
   decontrol and recontrol of cement, control,
   partial decontrol, full decontrol and price and
   levy control of sugar in India.

It has been the opinion of experts for some time in this context that a Committee of Economic and Juristic Experts be appointed to enquire into the utility of all existing controls, licensing and permit systems, and suggest elimination of such of these as are no longer considered necessary or have given rise to abuses and misfeasance.

The Wanchoo Committee added that the proposed committee may also suggest changes in law and procedures so as to ensure that the controls which are absolutely essential for the health of the economy are administered more effectively and with the least harassment to the public.

Increase in production

Control and rationing are of limited use in the fight against the black market in a situation of scarcity and their efficacy in a large measure depends primarily on the willingness and ability of the state to enforce them. As a matter of fact, it has been the experience in a number of countries that these measures themselves have been responsible in many cases for perpetuating the black market.

It has been sometimes said that increase in production to the level of demand, or even beyond, is the best antidote for the black market. This is a rather naive expectation. One essential aspect of black market strategy is to create conditions of artificial scarcity, by cornering and hoarding; or even by destroying part of the produce, to obtain the maximum profit-turnover.

Even if government would control production in entirety it would not ipso facto eliminate black marketing. Complete control in certain sectors of production would certainly establish government oligopoly, but that by itself may or may not increase production, and even if it did, it might not necessarily result in an increase in productivity. But once the produce is released in the market, nothing would prevent the forces in the black market to become active in their usual pattern of cornering, hoarding and strangulated black market sales, unless the state elected to enforce further restraints.

A few years back, the state had imposed in a developing country of South East Asia partial control system in the production of tapioca, in which black marketing has been rampant. Even if the entire firmament of production was taken over by the government, the black market could still hold its suzerainty by employing trip-boys, greasing the way through, and cornering bulk of the total produce.

Once it has done that, rest of the road is already mapped out for the market operatives, who would easily trot or canter along, as the situation would warrant, by playing on the forces of demand and supply, propensity to consume, liquidity preference and the level of purchasing power.

It is however difficult for the state, without changing the basic character of the economy, to wield complete control of the distribution system, as in the case of a totalitarian economy.

But if the forces of the black market and black money could at least be kept in leash by the government, an increase in production, or even an increase in the total supply, if necessary augmented by grants from abroad and bilateral imports, would certainly make higher supply possible at lesser prices in the market.[20] This is particularly relevant to a developing country, where agronomy holds the reins of the economy.[21]

It is expected that with a relentless drive spearheaded by the government under a well-conceived programme both against economic offences and proliferation of black market and black money on the one hand, and increase in production on the other, the trend in greater market-availability at lesser prices may first stabilize, and then gather momentum.

Meanwhile, the state has to demonstrate its willingness to play its part fully, and not by way of a flash-in-the-pan policy. Even today, in many a world economy, the government in regard to prices, is still relying more on exhortation than on specific action, but in a situation in which the old restraints based on fear no longer operate, moral suasion will not suffice. A many-splendoured strategy to enforce discipline in prices and distribution only can checkmate the contrary forces operating in the economy.[22]

Change in social values

The possibility of an overall change in social values, as a possible remedy for black market and black money, needs to be explored. Supposing that by means of a social revolution it was possible to achieve a complete change of values in which such vocations as medicine, law, teaching, auditing, architecture and similar other professions would command more social prestige and recognition than would mere possession of wealth with the nouveau riche in the black market and the smuggling-underworld, it may tend to work against further proliferations of the black market.

Secondly, the pace of such a social revolution would be faster if it was possible for the government to arrange a more or less equitable distribution of the basic needs of life.

In our opinion such a social revolution, however, can come, and would be of some use, only after the state has been able to liquidate the bastions of black market, black money and smuggling. As of now, the socially prestigious professions themselves, like law, medicine

and education, have been increasingly taking to tax
evasion and accumulation of black money and treasure,[23]
and therefore the chances of either their gaining in
social prestige and recognition or initiating such a
social revolution are rather remote at the present
moment.   This has in fact been a distressing phenomenon
in many a developed and underdeveloped countries, with
India being no exception.

Once, however, the government has been able to
strike at the roots of black market, black money, tax-
evasion and smuggling, will the time be opportune, in
the reformed atmosphere, (under which these crafts would
increasingly cease to pay and there would be reasonable
share for the people at least of the basic necessities
of life available in the country), to initiate such a
social revolution with a semblance of success.

Unearthing black money

A number of measures were recommended by the Direct
Taxes Enquiry Committee, India, in their Interim Report.
In their Final Report, the committee observed, "after
detailed deliberations and careful consideration, the
committee is still fully convinced about the efficiency
and feasibility of the measures recommended in the
Interim Report".

Before we discuss some of the recommendations we may
emphasize a very vital factor. Black money is the sheet-
anchor on which both black market and smuggling thrive.
If it is possible to unearth a substantial measure of
black money, both circulating and lying in shade, it will
greatly help in curbing the black market and liquidating
smuggling, on the one hand, and canalising the black
money and evaded income so unearthed into developmental
investments for planning economic growth, on the other.

DTEC did not lay much stress on the programmes of
voluntary disclosures as an effective syphon to pump out
black money. Besides, they thought that this scheme
would have deleterious effect on the level of compliance
on the tax-paying public and the morale of the administration.

The bearer-bond scheme again was considered a poor
substitute even to a disclosure scheme, as the former
can cover only black money which is not invested and is
lying in idle cash, and can therefore have no effect at
all on the black market, which stand and proliferate on
what may be called liquid black money.

Besides, the bearer bonds themselves will become,
as in case of licenses and permits, negotiable instruments of corruption and investment in black money. DTEC
therefore concluded that "the more we think of it, the
more we feel convinced that the so-called benefits
claimed for the bearer bond scheme are illusory".

If tax-evaders were to be allowed to assume the role

of social benefactors and were authorised to spend black
money in social, philanthropic or state-sponsored
ventures outside the orbit of taxation, DTEC observed,
as the above measures could actually mean, it would not
only detract from healthy canons of public finance, but
would also tend to provide a fillip to black marketing
and tax evasion.

Similar results would follow if a developing
economy like India were to follow a country in Europe and
another in Africa and allowed the opening of shadow
accounts pledged to a seal of secrecy. Measures such as
these would tend to perpetuate the black market and might
even hand over the reins of the economy to the forces of
black money. Same observation would apply to the parallel banking system of the smuggling underworld.[24]

What then would be the most effective measures that
government could adopt for raising the largest harvest of
black money ? We shall discuss these under different
heads in the subsequent paragraphs.

Searches and seizures

The Direct Taxes Enquiry Committee, India, laid the
maximum emphasis on searches and seizures as the most
potent weapon for unearthing black money. As a matter of
fact, the committee observed that "the power of search
under the Income Tax Act is a potent instrument in the
hands of the department to provide direct and clinching
evidence about tax evasion and the existence of black
money. The department should make an increasing use of
its powers of search and seizure in appropriate cases.[25]

The Wanchoo Committee recommended a number of
measures to make searches and seizures even more effective instruments than these are today for unearthing
black money. These recommendations are briefly summarised below:

1. A Commissioner or Assistant Commissioner of
   Income Tax should have power to authorise search
   and seizure, irrespective of whether the taxpayer assessed is in his jurisdiction or not.
2. The existing powers of search under the Income
   Tax Act should be extended to cover persons,
   vehicles and vessels.
3. The period for making such an order may be
   extended from the present ninety days to one
   hundred and eight days.
4. The law may be amended to permit retention of
   seized assets in order to meet the liability of
   interest and penalty, in addition to the tax,
   that may become due on the estimated undisclosed
   income.
5. The Income Tax Act[26] may be amended to provide
   that tho officer having jurisdiction over the
   case may apply for retention of the seized

material beyond the period of 180 days.
6. The law may be amended to raise a presumption to the effect that, unless proved to the contrary by the assessee, the assets which are seized in the course of a search will be deemed to represent his concealed income not so far taxed.
7. The law may be amended to provide a rebuttable presumption both for estimating the undisclosed income and also for prosecution of an assessee or an abettor.

In the years that followed, the Indian government has implemented some of these recommendations. In 1974-75, the Taxation Laws Amendment Act and certain other ordinances[27] were passed to this effect. Action under them, however, petered out by the end of 1975. It was also found that there was inadequate legal cover on the one hand, and on the other, the Ordinances gradually tended to become non-starters, in the absence of any endeavour on the part of the subsequent government to translate them into statutes and use them as effective arsenal of economic strategy. This also demonstrated, once again, that it was the will of the government to enforce a law that was even more important than the legislation by itself.

Qualitative demonetisation

Demonetisation,[28] by itself, can seldom be a solution to the problems of our kind. This will lead to multiple distortions in the economy, and also lead to difficulties for the law-abiding tax-payer. A qualitative demonetisation scheme however has some definite possibilities in this direction and deserves to be seriously considered.

Under this scheme, a ceiling may be determined for all real estate and liquid savings of all persons or groups of persons, in banks and vaults, lockers and hoards and other venues and media. Beyond this ceiling an assessee either would account for his possession with a twenty-five percent margin of difference, also to be explained in due course, or the possession beyond the ceiling would vest in the government and get diverted to the proposed State Refinance Corporation, suggested by us for investment of unearthed black money, towards the end of the chapter.

Such a scheme however needs to be examined by competent and acknowledged legal, financial and economic experts, before being considered, and the government may do well to set up a Committee of Experts on Qualitative Demonetisation.

Measures to fight tax evasion

Tax evasion leads to black money. Effectiveness of measures to fight tax evasion therefore will checkmate generation of black money. The latest official high-

power committee on tax-evasion in India was the Wanchoo
Committee, which has made valuable recommendations for
arresting the evasion. The present author, along with a
few other economic researchers in India like Ayub Syed,
Hannan Ezekiel and C.N. Vakil have probed the subject
further. From all these, a strategy against tax-evasion
could be built up on steps indicated in subsequent paragraphs.

1. Arousing social conscience
   Tax evasion can be dealt with effectively only
   if such measures are backed by strong public
   opinion against black money and tax evasion. In
   helping to build up such public opinion, the
   government can play a vital role. The foremost
   measure in this regard is denial of the privi-
   leges which are still available to tax evaders.
       Tax evaders should be disqualified for the
   purpose of getting awards and from holding any
   public elective office for a period of six years.
   No minister or officers of the government should
   attend functions sponsored or organised by tax
   evaders.
       A person who has been penalised or convicted
   for concealment of income/wealth should not be
   eligible to be a director or manager of a limited
   company for a period of six years. The Companies
   Act may be amended accordingly.
       Lists of taxpayers published by the govern-
   ment should include figures of income declared,
   income assessed and the tax payable. Such lists
   should, in addition to being published in the
   official gazette, be publicised in local papers
   and be also put up on notice boards in Income
   Tax offices.

2. Minimisation of controls and licenses
   All existing controls, licensing and permit
   systems should be reviewed by a Committee of
   Experts and such of these should be eliminated
   as are no longer considered necessary. These
   very often function as instruments of corruption
   and spin tax evasion and black money.[29]

3. Donations and allowances
   Donations by taxpayers, other than companies, to
   recognised political parties, and entertainment
   expenditure which is incurred primarily for the
   furtherance of the taxpayers' business and is
   directly related to its active conduct, should
   be allowed to be deducted upto ceilings
   prescribed.[30]
       The penalty clauses however should be
   extensively used to bag big offenders in tax
   evasion and unearth black money, rather than

small tax-evaders.
4. Vigorous prosecution

The Income Tax Department should completely
reorient itself to a more vigorous prosecution
policy in order to instil fear and wholesome
respect for the tax laws in the minds of the
tax-evaders. Further, where there is a reasonable chance of securing conviction, the tax
dodger should invariably be prosecuted.

The power to compound offences should be
used very sparingly. Flagrant cases of tax
evasion, particularly of persons in the high
income brackets, should be pursued relentlessly.
5. Intelligence and investigation

To cope with the increasing refinement and
sophistication of the techniques of tax evasion,
there is a need for a complete reorientation in
the Income Tax Department's approach to its
methods of intelligence and investigation. The
machinery of intelligence and investigation at
the command of the Department should be thoroug-
hly overhauled and streamlined to tackle adequately the menace of tax evasion.
6. Taxation of agricultural income

Agricultural income which is at present largely
outside the Central tax net, offers plenty of
scope for camouflaging black money. This therefore should be subjected to a uniform tax. In
fact, there is reason to believe that prosperity
in agriculture has not substantially spread out
to the tillers of the land, but has remained
confined to big farmers and landed families who
have managed to retain their ownership in the
names of different family-members, and that much
of their income is not as yet exposed to taxation.
7. Unexplained expenditure

A separate legal provision may be made to expose
unexplained expenditure to adequate taxation.
8. Substitution of sales-tax by excise duty

The best way to get over the problem posed by the
existing sales tax systems would be to replace
sales-tax levy on various commodities, as far as
possible, by additional duty of excise, but in
the selection of commodities, care should be
taken to minimise the cascading effect on prices,
particularly of commodities which are necessaries.
9. Compulsory maintenance of accounts

A provision may be introduced in the law,making
presentation of audited accounts mandatory in all
cases of business or profession where the sales/
turnover/receipts are Rs.50,000 or more.

10. Power of survey
    A new provision may be introduced to enable the
    income-tax officer to visit any premises of an
    assessee for the purpose of counting cash, veri-
    fying stocks, and inspecting accounts/documents.
11. Checking undervaluation
    It would be expedient for the government to
    assume powers to acquire immovable properties
    also in cases of understatement of cost of
    construction.
12. Foreign exchange violations
    An official study team appointed by the Govern-
    ment of India estimated in its report submitted
    in 1971 that the extent of leakage of foreign
    exchange is about Rs.240 crores yearly. This
    has been a gross underestimate. The Conserva-
    tion of Foreign Exchange and Prevention of
    Smuggling Act, 1974 (No.52 of 1974) needs to be
    suitably modified to prove an effective instru-
    ment in the hands of the government.
13. Tax evasion in film industry
    The law should be suitably enforced to arrest
    widespread tax evasion in the film industry by
    producers, directors, actors and actresses,
    music directors and play-back singers.
14. Fraudulent loans and investments
    Permanent account numbers and account payee
    cheques should serve as an effective check on
    bogus hundi loans. The Taxation Laws (Amend-
    ment) Act, 1971 discourages ghost holding of
    property. This was a step in the right direc-
    tion. The law, however, needs to be further
    tightened.

Concessional tax ordinances
    The Government offered late in 1975 an opportunity
for converting black money into white by paying income
tax at special rates ranging from 25 to 60 percent. The
offer, announced in the form of a Presidential Ordinance
on October 3, 1975, was open for a few months.[31] In
addition to payment of the tax, the declarant was
required to invest five percent of the disclosed income
in notified government securities, the proceeds of which
would be utilised for projects of high social priority.
    The benefit of the scheme was not available in the
case of smugglers and foreign exchange racketeers who
were detained or for whom detention orders were issued
under the Conservation of Foreign Exchange and Prevention of Smuggling Activities Act, 1974.(Cf.annexure 3).
    Two schemes of voluntary disclosures were tried in
1951 and 1965 apart from the demonetisation of high-
denomination notes immediately after the close of the
war in 1946 to bring into the tax net black money

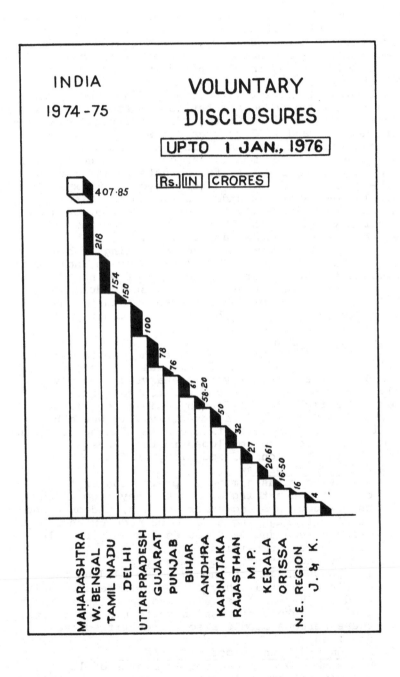

INDIA
1974-75

VOLUNTARY
DISCLOSURES

UPTO 1 JAN., 1976

Rs. IN CRORES

407·85

218

154
150

100

78
76

61

58·20

50

32

27

20·61

16·50

16

4

MAHARASHTRA
W. BENGAL
TAMIL NADU
DELHI
UTTAR PRADESH
GUJARAT
PUNJAB
BIHAR
ANDHRA
KARNATAKA
RAJASTHAN
M.P.
KERALA
ORISSA
N.E. REGION
J. & K.

144

earned during the war. Under the 1965 scheme announced
by the then Indian Finance Minister, T. T. Krishnamachari,
tax evaders could pay 60 percent of concealed income as
tax and bring the balance of 40 percent into their books.
These schemes put together resulted in a disclosure of
Rs.267 crores.

Although the Direct Taxes Enquiry (Wanchoo) Committee in 1971 had opposed any further schemes of voluntary
disclosures in the light of the 'disappointing' experience of the 1951 and 1965 schemes, it was possibly felt
that, together with various stringent measures taken
already to check black money, the government could afford
to give another opportunity for voluntary disclosures.

The results however have been beyond all expecta-
tions. The declarations under the voluntary disclosures
scheme have exceeded Rs.1,500 crores from the computations already made by the over-worked Income Tax authorities, as revealed on January 1, 1976.

The disclosures however gave an inkling of how
massive might be the extent of black money in India and
lent weight to the belief of a section of economists
that, voluntary disclosures, if implemented during a
temporary pause of otherwise stringent measures have
considerable capacity of siphoning black money particularly in a developing economy.[32]

Strategy against smuggling

In chapter 5, while investigating the racket of
smuggling in India, a detailed remedial strategy was
developed and their effectiveness analysed. We may
briefly summarise the different strategies required to
be used for a fight to the finish against smuggling.

Even though it would be repetitive, it would be
appropriate to sum up here, from chapter 5, the different
measures considered and developed in this thesis, for
liquidating the bastions of smuggling in India.[33]

1. Enforcement of law
   Intensive raids aiming at prevention of tax
   evasion, unearthing of black money from lockers,
   shadow accounts and other sources, hideouts and
   haunts of smuggling need to be made extensively.
   Raids on sea and land routes and airports also
   need to be intensified.
2. Arrest and detention of smugglers
   The known smugglers should be rounded up and
   detained, so that they cannot proliferate their
   trade. They have certain important links, which
   include racketeers, espionage agents and others;
   these persons should also be identified and
   detained.
3. Action under the process of the law
   Suits should be presented at courts of law
   against persons held under 1 and 2 above, and

their speedy convictions sought by the government.
For this purpose, even special courts and tribu-
nals should be set up for expeditious disposal of
cases and early convictions.

To what extent, voluntary surrenders by
smugglers should be exonerated from legal process
under the law of the land should be considered
very carefully, and not by considerations of
emotional amnesty.

4. Strengthening of hands of enforcement agencies
This is of extreme importance, not only to provide the legal cover, but also protection as necessary. Their job involves risks and hazards and
therefore should have adequate financial and
fringe-benefit incentives. The strength of such
agencies should also be increased as multiple and
frequent raids would be required.

5. Plugging loose ends of law
Appropriate and adequate enactments need to be
made to cover the loose ends of the different
statute laws like the Customs Act, Conservation
of Foreign Exchange and Prevention of Smuggling
Act etc. in India, for instance. As a matter of
fact, it would be wise to compile and pass a
comprehensive legislation relating to smuggling
and smugglers by land, sea and air, after a study
in depth by experts in economic jurisprudence.
There should be no hurry in repealing all anti-
smuggling acts and ordinances, but their tenabi-
lity in jurisprudence and desirability to the
economy, should be examined carefully. Those
which have already been repealed should also be
similarly scrutinised.

6. Seizure and attachment of properties
Properties in the shape of gold, jewellery,
bullion, lands, real estate, buildings, hotels,
motels, kiosks, bars, cinema houses, film studios
etc., owned by smugglers convicted or gone underground to escape the hands of the law, should be
seized, attached and then accredited to the
government.

7. Attachment of smugglers' banks and shadow
accounts
The real strength of the smuggling-rings lies in
their alternative banking system. A swift ordinance (followed by an enactment) for their
nationalisation and seizure would also appear
necessary to strike the final nails on the
coffin of smuggling.

Fraud and misfeasance
In order to tighten the auditor's watch against
fraud and misfeasance, a number of provisions should be

146

made legally binding in the management of companies as
also government departments and corporations.[34]

1. Auditors should not be allowed to render any
   service other than the professional service of
   auditing. When they do, they should cease to be
   audit firms.
2. No auditor should be allowed any position on the
   board of directors of any company as long as he
   continues to be a professional auditor. He
   should also not be given a position in the
   management other than as auditor.
3. Any complaint on the accuracy of audit by 10
   percent of the shareholders (present and voting)
   at a general body meeting should be compulsorily
   followed up by an independent investigation.
4. In order to reduce concentration of audit business among selected firms a system of rotation
   should be followed whereby no audit firm is
   allowed to audit the accounts of the same client
   for more than three years in five years.
5. As a general rule, a supervisory audit should be
   undertaken every three years by an audit firm
   other than the one contractually employed as
   auditor of a particular company.[35]

Investment of unearthed resources

Conversion of black money unearthed and evaded
income retrieved into authorised investment for development programme merits serious consideration. During the
last few years, in sporadic spurts of offensives, the
Indian government, for instance, had seized and attached
black money, evaded-income, black-money treasures and
smuggled gold and commodities worth several hundred
crores of rupees. If a well-coordinated drive is again
launched and relentlessly continued almost as a permanent strategy by the government, the seizures would
total into staggering proportions of confiscated
currency, treasures and assets.

We discussed earlier how such concepts in the
evolution of developmental planning in India as 'plan
holiday' and 'core plan' have developed mainly because
of shortage of investment-finance. The unearthed black
money and retrieved income, treasures and valuables,
properties attached and 'going concerns' taken over by
the government should now be canalised into essential
investment channels.

It is our suggestion that for this purpose the
central government in India should set up, as a subsidiary to the State Bank of India, a State Refinance
Corporation, in which should vest all unearthed money and
income retrieved, gold and jewellery, treasures and
valuables seized, as also all properties and real
estates attached and all going concerns including firms

and factories, hotels and motels, kiosks and bars,
cinema houses and film studios taken over by the
government.

It will be for this Corporation to attend to the
legal aspects of such seizures and acquisition and their
further disposal or continuity. At the same time, this
Corporation will determine the channels of developmental
investments out of the huge money and assets that would
be placed at the disposal of the said Corporation. It
has to be ensured that such seized wealth does not find
its way into 'party funds', a manifest method of corruption in public life at political level in many countries.

The Corporation, however, should not get bogged
down in a wide network of investments, and should on the
contrary concentrate on development investment in only
two selected sectors of plan-investment:

1. Agriculture, by bringing more land under cultivation, by arranging ryotwari bandobast in such a
   way that we may have a string of large scale
   collective or state-owned farms, of not less than
   100 hectares each, and by modernising methods of
   cultivation all over the country.
2. Geological and geophysical surveys and mining,
   by undertaking and financing new surveys of areas
   and mineral belts and beds of oil and petroleum,
   and undertaking or financing, at least in the
   beginning, mining in new sectors and drilling of
   new flows.

Similar steps are recommended for a number of other
countries, particularly with developing economy, even
though the strategy should be delineated with care and
could be different in matters of detail for different
countries.

Epilogue

Summarising from the earlier chapters, we may now
draw our conclusions. Many factors, starting from
certain compelling considerations of plan strategy,
effects of wars, droughts and crop failures, to debt-
servicing, diminishing returns on imports and less
favourable exchange balances, have been responsible for
a galloping price spiral in India since independence.
But one major decideratum has been the forces unleashed
by black market, black money, national and international
smuggling and drainage in foreign exchange resources.
Hand in hand with the price spiral moved the curves of
inflation and money supply, or vice versa.

The country appears to have been caught up in the
midst of a hyperinflation, with the economy being sapped
away by the evil forces of corruption, profiteering,
black market, smuggling and black money, tax evasion,
hoarding and adulteration giving a hand.

It has been the endeavour in this treatise

148

INDIAN ECONOMY
NET NATIONAL PRODUCT

PERCENTAGE RATE OF GROWTH
(WEIGHTED)

to formulate plans for arresting these trends and to
devise programmes for cleansing the economy from the
pressures let loose by the black market, black money,
smuggling and other economic offences in India and a
number of other countries suffering from similar economic
malaise.

There is really no point in preaching the gospel to
those who haunt the black alleys of the economy and try
to transcend their image with respectability bought by
sheer ill-gotten money-power. Their bastions have to be
liquidated and their anti-growth manoeuvres checkmated.

This is not possible by appeals or exhortations.
This can be achieved mainly by the state which, arming
itself with adequate juristic, financial, fiscal and
executive authorities, should mean to take action and
demonstrate in actual practice not only its willingness
but also its capability to wage a relentless vendetta
against economic offenders and their bases and vaults.

There is no other way out. While imaginative
economic planning will initiate strategies towards growth,
a continued and comprehensive war against the reins of
black market, black money and economic offences will
release resources for plan-oriented investment and growth
and mitigate trends towards manifestations of wide
disparities in income and distribution.

Neither full economic license nor complete economic
regimentation will be necessary in the struggle against
black market and other allied pursuits; and appropriately
conceived governmental measures, planned and legislated
with economic and legal expertise, and, more than most,
executed with sincerity and adroitness, will certainly
achieve the desired objectives, within the professed
framework of democracy.

NOTES

1. Clay - Economics for the General Reader.
Cole - Some Relations between Political &
Economic Theory (1934).
Dimcock - Business and Government (1949), Henry
Holt and Co. Inc., New York.
2. Report of Taxation Enquiry Committee, Vol.I,
1953-54, Chapter IX, page 177.
3. Steiner - Government's Role in Economic Life
(1953); Mcgraw-Hill, New York.
4. Ellis - The Economic Way of Thinking; American
Economic Review, Vol. 40, No.1, March 1950. Also 3 ibid.
5. Steiner - ibid.
Boulding - A Reconstruction of Economics (1950);
John Willey & Sons Inc., New York.
6. Quoted in The Independent Regulatory Commissions
by Robert E. Cushman; Oxford University Press, London.

150

7. Lin Yutang - The Wisdom of Confucius (1939);
Carlton House, Inc., New York. Also 3 ibid.
8. Mrs. Indira Gandhi, in her address before the
reconstituted Planning Commission of India in mid-1980.
9. S.K. Ray - Economics of Black Market Profits;
Economic Times, New Delhi, November 26, 1974.
10. S.K. Ray - The Profiteering Curve; Business
Standard, May 9, 1977.
11. The consequent market behaviour has been explained in chapter 2. Summarising, the commodity thereafter
would become available only at certain times, or certain
places, or to certain favoured customers. The price
however would be no more the concern of the buyer, but
would be what would suit the black marketeer, and the
price will be governed by the principle of caveat emptor.
12. Jather & Beri - Indian Economics, Vol.I (1949);
Oxford University Press, Calcutta.
13. The situation has been depicted by Boulding in
his Economic Analysis graphically.
14. Boulding - ibid.
15. Boulding - ibid.
16. Chapter 2, Economics of Profiteering.
17. Final Report of DTEC (1971).
18. Final Report of DTEC (1971), Summary of Observations and Recommendations.
19. Final Report of DTEC (1971).
20. S.K. Ray - Price Regulatory Measures; Business
Standard, Calcutta, May 3,1978.
21. S.K. Ray - The Profiteering Curve; Financial
Express, Bombay, May 9, 1977.
22. S.K. Ray - Inflation and Growth; Business
Standard, Calcutta, January 10 & 11, 1980.
23. Final Report of DTEC, 1971, Chapter 2.
24. Ayub Syed - Smugglers in the net: What now?;
Illustrated Weekly of India, Bombay, November 1974.
25. Para 2.39 of the Final Report of DTEC, 1971.
26. Section 132(8) of the Income Tax Act, 1961.
27. Many of these ordinances and acts passed under
them were struck down when the Union Government at
New Delhi changed.
28. As an economic weapon, demonetisation by and
large still remains a theoretical proposition.
29. The Central Bureau of Investigation in India in
1975 caught 120 firms which had wrongly utilised over
500 import licenses valued at more than Rs.6 crores
obtained under the category of 'actual users'. Investigations during the last three years from 1972 also
resulted in bringing to book 80 firms which had
'succeeded' in obtaining 140 licenses valued at Rs.1
crore by 'misrepresenting facts or by producing forged
documents'. (Report in Hindustan Times, New Delhi,
October 2, 1975).

30. S.K. Ray - <u>Extent of Corruption In The Economy</u>;
The Hindu, Madras, June 25, 1979. (cf. Annex. 3).

31. The Concessional Tax Ordinance, 1975.

32. The present author has voiced this opinion
repeatedly in the Indian press in his discourses on
economics and public finance.

33. Chapter 5, <u>The Labyrinth of Smuggling</u>.

34. Most of these were suggested by Dr. D.K.
Rangnekar, formerly Editor of Economic Times, when he
was a member of the Direct Taxes Enquiry Committee, India.
Dr. Rangnekar is presently Editor of Business Standard,
Calcutta.

35. S.K. Ray - <u>Management & Company Affairs</u>;
The Management Accountant, Calcutta; May 1979.

11

A Quintessence

Very little discussion is available on the black market in economic literature. There are some tentative discourses by Plumtre, Boulding and Kalechi, but these are in nature nothing more than peripheral. In the context of black marketing having since become a way of life in the Indian sub-continent, research on this subject in applied economics in the Indian situation has become imperative.

Theoretical format

In India, particularly during the last few decades, forces of black market, black money, smuggling and such other economic offences have wielded a substantial control over the economy, and have played havoc with the standard of living of the people and economic pursuits of the government. The black market has become a force to reckon with, and certainly deserves a complete socio-economic investigation. Such an analysis, in the background of the Indian economy, if conducted on a pragmatic, didactic and realistic way, will be utilitarian as a socio-economic exploration.

While a theory of the black market may take shape in the trail of the Robinson-Chamberlin-Triffin sequence of the theories of imperfect competition, our analysis, instead of drawing its substance from arbitrary assumptions of neo-classical economics, may turn to more empirical and fruitful methods. It will recognise the richness and variety of all concrete cases, and tackle each problem with due deference. More advantage will be taken of all relevant factual information and less reliance will be placed on a mere resort to the pass-key of general theoretical assumptions.

After having established the nature of the concept, and the need and method of research, our endeavour will be to unravel the depth, structure, organisation and objectives of the black market in India, its link with black money and other economic offences, their mode of operation, and to determine their socio-economic repercussions.

It is also our objective, in the background of a discussion of strategies so far evolved in different shades of economic systems, to filter and recommend remedial measures best suited to the Indian economy.

Profiteering

The edifice of the Indian black market is unsatis-fied demand. While this is so, black market manoeuvres do always throw the black market supply curve to the left of the normal supply curve. Black marketing is no freshman's job, but requires considerable skill and understanding of the market-behaviour. It also involves substantial risk and cost, particularly while trying to hijack the price-spiral and while on the errand of profiteering.

These elements will by and large determine the level of supply and pricing in the black market, in relation to demand and purchasing power. Their inter-action however is artificially adjusted every now and then by the black marketeer in order to achieve the maximum turnover on his outlay. How this is done in the work-a-day life can be illustrated by practical investi-gations of the market situation, as has been done exten-sively during the course of the present research.

We know of the concept of profit optimisation, which is the guiding criterion of open-market behaviour. In the case of the black market, there is an outright changeover of the objective from profit optimisation to profit maximisation, by any or all means. Profit maxi-misation, or profiteering, will be conditioned by the forces of increasing risk, cost and uncertainty in the black market.

The necessary margin between cost and price required for black market profiteering may be kept by artificial contraction of supply in relation to demand, through hoarding or sealed production or such other devices, or by tapping the inflationary fever of purchasing power, through effective manipulation of supply or liquidity or both. In either case, there is an artificial scarcity of supply in relation to both consumption-propensity and liquidity-preference.

The result is a serious gap between supply and demand of a commodity, and in more senses than one, this gap determines the level of prices in the black market and the extent of profiteering.

Profiteering is not only the principal but the sole objective for the black market operators today. Profit-eering in the black market, as an economic phenomenon, is achieved by sponsoring an inter-action in the curves of (unsatisfied) demand and (restricted) supply with first a multiplier and then an accelerator effect, aided further by a multiplicity of commodity, and the wave of

the price spiral.
Black money
Kaldor's was a pioneering effort in estimating the
ranges of black money and tax evasion in India. That
was in 1955. On the basis of his computations, which
were sufficiently useful as a first approximation,
Kaldor estimated an amount of public taxation lost to
exchequer of the order of Rs.200 to 300 crores.

The link of black money with the black market is
intimate. The huge amount does not keep lying in the
shade, but is adroitly transferred through multiple
channels to the black market and the smuggling underworld
to spin money back. Out of Rs.300 crores of tax-evaded
black money estimated by Kaldor, in 1957, one-third
would have been in storage, and two-third mostly in
secretive circulation.

The Direct Taxes Enquiry Committee (DTEC), generally
called the Wanchoo Committee, produced their interim
report in 1970 and final report in 1971. The Committee
continued Kaldor's tentative research, and gave a more
or less authoritative estimate of the extent of black
money in the Indian economy.

Black money denotes not only unaccounted currency
which is either hoarded or is in circulation outside the
disclosed trading channels, but also its investment in
gold, jewellery and precious stones made secretly, and
even investments in lands and buildings and business
assets over and above the amounts shown in the books of
accounts.

DTEC has emphasised the dual nature of the Indian
economy. Thus there is an official economy, functioning
on the basis of the official monetary system, and a
parallel economy, based on black money, black market and
the underworld of economic offences, operating a parallel
banking system and all the time at war with government's
economic policies and pursuits.

Working from the conclusions of the Wanchoo
Committee, and allowing for the white money factor, and
the accepted rate of proliferation, the estimate of
black money in India in 1975-76 would be a couple of
thousand crores, in absolute terms; it would be substantially higher in terms of money value of the treasures,
properties and transactions they cover.

Today, in mid-1980, it should be substantially
higher even in absolute terms. By 1976, around Rs.2,000
crores were netted in the voluntary disclosure scheme
alone.

The impact and implication of these figures are
profound and staggering. The operation of black-money
economy has already upset the momentum of our development
in India to a substantial extent.

It has been responsible for generation of such

distress-concepts in the governance of the Indian
economy as 'core plan' and 'plan holiday', due to shortage of adequate finance to support the plan-programmes.
This is a matter of great pity, considering the huge
amounts resting in the folds of black money that could
have seen India through several successive ambitious
five-year plans, with little or no recourse to deficit
financing and international debt-servicing.

Stages and sectors

The black market has a vertical structure, with
successive, allied and frequently inter-linked stages.
Each such stage or tier again has several horizontal
sectors, complementary to each other. Each sector
functions with the common objective of profiteering.

Our study may reckon with the organisation and the
financial structures of the black market, which are
different only in functional attributes, but are otherwise coextensive and inter-dependent.

The analysis also takes stock of the research made
on the subject by different official and non-official
committees or institutions like the Indian Toxicological
Research Centre and the Direct Taxes Enquiry Committee.
It also probes into the position of the economic offences
vis-a-vis the law of the land.

While examining the financial structure of the
black market, it has been found that the most important
source of money supply for the black market is black
money. Black money is also the source for financing
national and international smuggling. There is also a
drainage of white money into black market.

Smuggling

There have been several official and unofficial
estimates of the extent of smuggling in India. According
to official sources, smuggling in India today is foreign
trade without government sanction and running of a
parallel central bank; the turnover of this bank
reportedly operating a forceful clandestine network is
estimated at Rs.2,000 crores according to one non-
official estimate.

There are three objectives in perpetration of which
smuggling is done; conversion of foreign exchange, export
of contraband and import of contraband.

It has been exposed that there is an umbrella of
protection on the smuggling underworld provided by degenerate elements in legal profession, social services and
politics, the trend having started as a British legacy.

It has been delineated that in order to liquidate
smuggling in India, steps that would be required to be
taken, would relate to enforcement of law, detention of
smugglers, action under the process of law, strengthening the machinery for enforcement, plugging the loose
ends of law, seizure of properties and, finally, nationa-

lisation of smugglers'- banks and seizure of shadow
accounts.

Price behaviour
An analysis of the price situation has to take stock
of the structural imbalances in the economy, as also the
inflationary, currency-circulation and investment situation. The position regarding development-expenditure,
budgetary gaps, balance of payments, national and international borrowings and debt-servicing is also extremely
relevant.

Inflation, it has been analysed, is a socially
costly and economically wasteful means of increasing
investment.

While there was no dearth of economic resources to
finance a few successive plans, this lay largely in the
shape of black money and in the labyrinth of the black
market and international smuggling, and the country had
to get submerged into an avalanche of public debt and
foreign-debt servicing. What was worse, the growing
forces of black market, smuggling and black money made
costing of expansion and growth to jump and did eat
away plenty of our investible surplus.

Against this background, an extensive analysis
has been made in the present research into the behaviour
patterns of general, wholesale and retail price-levels
in the Indian sub-continent since independence, over the
four plan periods, identifying the seasonal, sectional
and commodity-wise characteristics of prices.

Together with an analysis of the forces relating to
the supply of agricultural and industrial commodities,
the forces of demand, population, investment, inflation
and money-supply as affecting the price-levels have also
been delineated in our analysis.

In the play of prices the elongating shadow of the
forces unleashed by black market, black money, smuggling
and other economic offences have also been identified.

Finally, an appraisal of the economic situation has
been made vis-a-vis the state policies on prices, money-
supply, inflation and growth.

Fraud and misfeasance
As techniques of operation, such activities as
fraud and defalcation, embezzlement and misfeasance, are
not exactly in the category of the black market. But as
manifestations of distorted human behaviour, they are
really not far removed.

Internal check is an antidote for frauds, but this
does not absolve the auditor of his responsibilities for
protecting the interests of shareholders and taxpayers
against the perpetration of frauds. The extent of such
responsibility has been determined mainly through a
string of important law cases, apart from whatever little
written or unwritten law is available on the subject.

As in case of black market or black-money deals or smuggling, fraud and misfeasance are also committed by degenerate elements in the employ of government departments or companies, or by likeminded persons aiding and abetting with them, or both.

Red eyes of the law and the efficiency of the enforcement machinery are two deterrents. Another equally important preventive deterrent is the effectiveness of internal check and auditing, and to that end, the liability and responsibility shouldered by the auditor.

Corruption in public life

Corruption is not exclusive to developing countries, where however, their effects on the national economy take a much heavier toll than in case of economically advanced nations.

An analysis has been made in the present research of the evolution of corruption in India from the ancient Hindu period to the present time. Since the second world war, however, corruption in Indian economic life has blossomed in hundred myriad ways.

There have been committees on corruption, like the Santhanam and Kripalani Committees; but an appraisal of their reports indicated that these had depicted the trends of corruption rather than providing any clinical assessment of the extent, nature and depth of corruption and its multiple and myriad proliferation.

A metropolitan survey on corruption, based on 500 interviews, conducted by the Indian Institute of Public Opinion, has been chronicled, tabulated and evaluated in the course of the research. The results derived from the survey are indicative of the general trend of affairs in our country, the modality of corruption in the national economy, and the resultant extent of cynicism, frustration and resignation generated amongst the people.

Where do we go from here ? How do we tackle the monster of corruption ? ... Attempts have been made in the treatise to find answers to these questions. It has been our conclusion that corruption in public life is basically a political evil, and therefore only political solutions will prove effective.

A country may survive petty corruption, but the sharks and octopuses of corruption have to be fettered. A naive witch-hunt for small shellfish-eaters will be of little consequence.

Conclusions and suggestions

The socio-economic consequences of black market, black money, smuggling and other economic offences have been extensively discussed in appropriate places in the course of the research. Economists are alive to them and are also unanimous that these must be contained or liquidated to salvage the economy from their stranglehold. There is however much controversy as to how this should be actually accomplished.

The effectiveness of various remedial measures have been analysed at length. The discussions and analyses have covered, _inter alia_, price regulation and control, rationing, consumers' resistance movement, change in social values and increase in production, on the one hand, and measures for unearthing black money and fighting tax evasion, working out a strategy against smuggling and fighting fraud, misfeasance and corruption, on the other.

Incidentally, concepts like qualitative demonetisation have also been discussed, the strategies outlined and executed by the government analysed and their effectiveness quantified. The jurisprudence in support of the drive has also been elaborately examined.

A State Refinance Corporation has been proposed as a subsidiary to the State Bank of India to monitor the investment of the huge assets and resources unearthed as a result of the drive. The government, however, has to take care to see that the police and enforcement machineries do not themselves tend to take to corrupt practices.

A new horizon is being opened up, and it depends on the people and the government whether India should quicken the march or take to slow pedestrian walk. There need be a new awakening, together with an adequate economic programme, fortified by statutory, administrative and economic weapons, for the country to tackle the menace of multiple economic offences.

Neither full economic license nor complete economic regimentation will be necessary in the struggle against black market and other allied pursuits; and appropriately conceived governmental measures, planned and legislated with economic and legal expertise and executed with sincerity and adroitness, will achieve the desired objectives, within the framework of democracy.

Annexure 1
SHOULD ECONOMICS PLAY SECOND FIDDLE?

*Reproduced from an article by the author published in
Financial Express, Bombay, December 20, 1980.*

Economics during the last few decades has shown a
propensity to get itself extensively enmeshed in mathematics. What started with some branches of economics
like demography and statistics, has now swept over a large
portion of monetary and applied economics, including
planning and development.

It is necessary to appreciate the extent of this
trend and its impact on the study and research in
different branches of economics generally and the basic
theory in particular.

A scholarly criticism of such a school of thought
started in Keynes' heyday, and while discussing a group
of economic variables used in the Pigovian literature,
Keynes found it necessary to caution against extreme
mathematisation of economic analysis.

The trend towards large-scale mathematisation of
economics has increasingly confined economic dissertations to what may be called a non-competitive group of
researchers. This became manifest particularly in the
later post-Keynesian period and, more than most, in the
works of monetary and pricing theorists. Some of the
consumers' surplus theorists have also woven their thesis
completely into intricate mathematical models and
presentations.

Keynes and Pigou

It was in his General Theory of Employment, Interest
and Money that Keynes cautioned against the excessive
tendency of mathematising the study of economics. He
said that too large a proportion of recent mathematical
economics was mere concoction ... which allowed the
author to lose sight of the complexities and inter-
dependencies of the real work in a maze of presentations
and symbols.

Keynes has always emphasised that there is no point
in formulating a theory on a pyramid of presumptions,
both at the base as also at the tiers and the apex,

161

where such presumptions are dissociated from economic
variables highly relevant to the economic phenomenon,
and which such economic theory aims to explain.

One cannot say that such an approach was unique to
Pigou, for there were a number of other illustrious
economists who also tended to do so. But while the
latter had never meant to say that their theories
covered all possible economic variables relevant to a
theory, a large portion of Pigou's theories (of
employment and wages), in the opinion of Keynes, was
more or less an exercise in simplicity and assumptions.

It is true that economists like Marshall and Kahn
were exploring new concepts of economics and laying down,
at the same time, the infrastructure of economic
research. They did not know of all or many of the
economic forces at play, and many of the economic
variables as yet remained to be identified; but they
did underscore the exploratory approach in their
dissertations.

Keynes took up cudgels against extreme mathematisation of economics, for the first time, while writing a
critique on Pigou's treatise, Theory of Unemployment.
According to Keynes, we might regard Pigou's volume as
a non-causative investigation into the functional
relationship which determined what level of real wages
would correspond to any given level of employment.

But his theory was not able, according to Keynes,
of telling us what determined the actual levels of
employment; and on the problem of involuntary unemployment it had no direct bearing. These were, in fact,
only two of the main inadequacies that Keynes had
spotlighted in his criticism, while he had referred to
a host of others.

A maze of symbols

The main charge of Keynes against the Pigovian
theory of employment has been the alleged attempt to
detract from the absence of adequate causative investigation, in a mathematical cobweb, with symbols and models
galore. Keynes has been rather merciless in upbraiding
the Pigovian mathematical formulations. What Keynes has
criticised in his magnum opus is nothing short of a
veritable demolition of what he thought was a trend to
confine economic research within a rigidly mathematical
outfit.

A number of economists have, in later years,
supported Keynes to the hilt, and a few of them
established by didactic analysis that Keynes was correct
in his conclusion about too much reliance on mathematical
models in the formulation of economic theories and their
subsequent applications.

According to the Keynesian school of thought, the
pitfalls of pseudo-mathematical methods which can make

no progress except by making everything a function of a
single variable, and assuming that all the partial
differentials vanish, could not be better illustrated
than in Pigou's work. "For it is no good to admit later
that there are, in fact, other variables, and yet to
proceed without rewriting upto that point".
Economic laws
        Economics from the time of Marshall to that of
Kuznets has been considered basically a study in humani-
ties. A part of economic research during the last few
decades, taking a leaf from Pigou, however, has made it
a study more in econometrics than in economics.
        Increasing recourse has been taken to contain
economic laws within finely chiselled propensities. The
age-old belief that economic laws cannot be axiomated
with physical laws has been largely ignored.
        In order to fit economic theories into statistical
or mathematical models, a large number of assumptions
were made and economic laws reduced to the category of
straight-jacket norms of algebra or arithmetic.
        In this category of economic research, too much has
been made of the sanctity of economic laws. The flexible
economic law of yesterday has been made to take the shape
of a geometric theorem, so to say, in order to mathema-
tise the framework of monetary management and fiscal
policy, public finance and plans for development.
        In this context, the present author has been a
rather solitary economic theorist in India who throughout
criticised the strict and archaic adherence to economic
laws and championed the need for flexibility of approach
to economic phenomena, particularly in the formulation
of policies on planning for development.
        The extent to which the trend towards presumptive
mathematisation has crystallised is no more in the nature
of isolated scholarship. The phenomenon today covers
a substantial part of post-Keynesian economic thought,
at least during the last few decades.
        The trend has had two immediate effects. First,
fundamental economics is fast becoming a preserve of
the mathematical specialist. Even brilliant exponents
of economics, whose mainstay has not been mathematics,
not infrequently do feel like outcastes as far as
today's exposition of economic phenomena is concerned.
This has happened not only in government circles like the
planning and tariff commissions and economic study-groups,
but also in the mainstream of economic scholarship.
        Secondly, the application of economics in today's
finance, commerce, fiscal and tariff policies, international trade, planning and development, has become
presumptive rather than pragmatic. Plans are being often
worked out in different areas of economic activities
based on conclusions derived from a number of mathematical

164

models, which themselves have frequently been worked out from predetermined norms formulated on the basis of geometric, quantific, statistical, demographic, or such other mathematical appraisals alone.

A casualty

This is all right, as far as it goes. Trouble has arisen from the fact that in many cases these models have been raised on inadequate investigation of economic phenomena, which were irrationally simplified by casting away a number of variables on which researches have not been made, and taking recourse to presumptions in respect of some others.

In all such cases, flexibility has been the immediate casualty. A typical mathematical formulation of this nature resembles a building where it is difficult to demolish a wall or a pillar without demolishing the entire structure or a substantial part thereof.

In economics as a humanitarian science, in the sense we understand it, changes in the socio-economic phenomena, or in the relevant substantive or peripheral economic laws, have been duly reckoned with, and adjustments made in the ideation of the economic theory and the ramification of planning and development.

Contrary to many of today's mathematical projections of economic thought, economics in the humanitarian sense used to be based on a continuous process of exploration, and, let us admit, used to make room for adjustments in the theory as also in the dynamics of development.

It was not considered that once an economic law was given, it was perfect and that it would determine all future developments based on it, or in pursuance of it. The law itself was subjected to continuous research and would often give way to a new law, if found necessary, and draw fresh findings and conclusions. It has not been, as it frequently is in today's mathematical economics, that a law was supreme once and for all.

A controversy

Today's mathematical economics is fast becoming a science in which we are often increasingly trying to automatise knowledge, and are thereupon making doctrines subservient to norms, trends or whatever we might call them.

Even in the formulation of our planning strategies, through economic models based on mathematics, we frequently do arrive at certain conclusions, however divorced from realities the same might be. Even faced with subsequent changes in circumstances, we cannot distrust our house of cards — the mathematical model based largely or partly on assumptions. This is because of the mental and theoretical allegiance to certain assumed mathematical premises, on which the theory or the thesis was initially built up.

This experience is becoming more manifest in developing economies where even the study and application of humanitarian economics has not reached a high degree of development. In these countries, cultivation of economics is rather peripheral in government establishments or commissions while even in the universities and research institutes, it seldom manifests itself in independent works of authority.

Taking shelter under mathematical economics, research, particularly in these countries, frequently tends to become more or less an exercise in arithmetic based on norms and presumptions. In the applied branches of economics such as planning and development, tariffs and public finance, this has often precipitated a host of distortions in the economy with every change in the perspective. It was against this trend that the present author has repeatedly cautioned both the scholars and the planners.

A lot of naivete has permeated economic analysis and it is being increasingly felt that an economic theory needs to be built more on a complete investigation of economic variables rather than a host of presumptions, frequently window-dressing the latter by mathematisation.

Even in fundamental economics, a charlatan tendency to overlook vital factors should be deprecated. In formulating an economic theory on a fiscal or monetary policy, as the present author has repeatedly emphasised, there is no objection to the use of mathematics to build up the premises or to reach the conclusions, but not to partial or complete exclusion of an objective analysis of all the relevant economic forces at work.

Annexure 2
COMPUTATION OF BLACK MONEY IN INDIA

*Reproduced from the Final Report of the Direct
Taxes Enquiry Committee, Government of India,
published in 1971.*

As regards the extent of tax evasion and black
money, the present study is based on an adoption of the
Kaldor method, with suitable modifications, bearing in
mind the structural changes in the economy and certain
other ancillary developments.

The conclusion of this study is that the assessable
non-salary income and the actually assessed non-salary
income for the financial year 1961-62 were Rs.2,686
crores and Rs.1,875 crores respectively. Accordingly,
the income which escaped tax for that year would appear
to be of the order of Rs.811 crores.

In late 'sixties

In order to ascertain the position for the
financial year 1965-66 (assessment year 1966-67), being
the latest year for which detailed revenue statistics
are available with us, we arrived at the assessable
non-salary income for that year, on the basis that
was adopted for 1961-62 financial year at a figure of
Rs.4,027 crores. This is indicated in Table A.2.1.

Applying the ratio of evaded income to the
assessable non-salary income of 1961-62 to the assessable
non-salary income of 1965-66, the evaded income for
1965-66 works out to Rs.1,216 crores. However, we
should like to qualify these estimates for three reasons:

1. The income which can be related to the assessment
   year 1966-67 does not fully represent the
   income generated in or related to the financial
   year 1965-66. Accounting years and varying dates
   and a certain backlog are also involved in routine
   assessments. Larger income cases needing more
   scrutiny may not always be completed within the
   relevant years and many such cases may have been
   carried forward.

2. The national income figures cannot be strictly
   compared with incomes assessed because the
   Indian Income Tax Act allows a large number of

167

Table A.2.1

Sectorwise distribution of assessable non-salary
income for 1965-66 (assessment year 1966-67)

| | National income | | Assumed propor- tion of non- salary income above exempt- ion limit (in per- centage) | Assess- able non- salary income |
Sector	Total salary income	Non- salary income		
1. Mining and quarrying	94	140	60	84
2. Manufacturing (a)	1,890	2,310	60	1,386
3. Railways and Communications	416	97	–	–
4. Other transport systems	223	222	60	133
5. Trade, hotels and restaurants	445	1,784	70	1,249
6. Banking and insurance	245	90	100	90
7. Public administration and Defence	1,040	260	100	260
8. Miscellaneous (b)	–	1,651	50	825
Total	4,353	6,554	–	4,027
9. Agricultural	1,575	8,271	–	–
Grand Total	5,928	14,825		

(Rupees in crores)

Notes

(a) Includes large-scale, small-scale and
    construction industries, electricity, gas,
    water supply, etc.
(b) Includes real estate ownership and other
    services.

exemptions and deductions (for example, casual
and non-recurring receipts, income of new
industrial undertakings and priority industries
and deduction for development rebate, etc.). No
adjustment is possible in the case of such
exemptions and deductions.
3. No adjustment has been made in respect of
certain incomes which are subject to income tax
twice due to provisions of the income-tax law.
For example, the income of a firm is taxed also
in the hands of its partners. Due to lack of
data, no adjustment has been made in respect of
such items also.

Even after taking all these limitations into
account and after making rough adjustments on the basis
of information available, the estimated income on which
tax has been evaded would probably be Rs.700 crores and
Rs.1,000 crores for the years 1961-62 and 1965-66
respectively. Projecting this estimate further to
1968-69 on the basis of the percentage of increase in
the national income from 1961-62 to 1968-69 (during
which period the national income increased nearly by
100 percent), the income on which tax was evaded for
1968-69 can be estimated at a figure of Rs.1,400 crores.

As regards the extent of tax evasion, we find that
the average rate of tax on the income assessed for
1965-66 was around 25 percent.

Approximations

But considering that the size of the problem of
black money and tax evasion has grown over the years
and tax evasion is more widely practised at higher
levels of income, it would be appropriate to adopt the
rate of tax applicable to evaded income at not less
than 33 1/3 percent for 1968-69.

On this basis, the extent of income-tax evaded
during 1968-69 would be of the order of Rs.470 crores,
being one-third of Rs.7,000 crores for 1968-69. It may,
however, be emphasised that the amount of tax-evaded
income for the year 1968-69 is only approximate, based
on certain assumptions about which substantial difference
of opinion exists for want of adequate data. In addition,
it may be better to dispel a popular impression that the
tax-evaded income is all lying hoarded which can be
seized by the authorities; much of it has been either
converted into assets or spent away in consumption or
else is in circulation in undisclosed business dealings.

Annexure 3
ORDINANCES AGAINST SMUGGLING

*A resume of ordinances passed in 1975 by
the central government of India against
smugglers and their activities.*

An ordinance was passed amending the Anti-Smuggling
Act of July 1, 1975. This ordinance set out measures for
proclaiming smugglers who went underground as <u>absconders</u>.
It also contained provisions for arranging seizure of
properties of smugglers, including those of proclaimed
absconders.
<u>Amendments</u>
It was later decided by an amendment to the
ordinance that as far as smugglers were concerned, it
was not necessary to indicate grounds for detention.
Later, another amendment prescribed that such detentions
were not justiciable.
Persons detained in connection with prevention of
smuggling activities under the Conservation of Foreign
Exchange and Prevention of Smuggling Activities Act,
1974, need not be given the grounds for detention,
according to an ordinance promulgated by the President
on July 1, 1975, amending the Act.
Under the ordinance, the cases of such persons
need not be referred to an Advisory Board during the
currency of a declaration by the detaining authority
that the detention is necessary in dealing effectively
with the emergency.
It has been provided in the amending ordinance
that where an order of detention is based on two or
more grounds, such order shall be deemed to have been
made separately on each of such grounds.
Thus an order shall not be deemed to be invalid
or inoperative merely because one or some of the
grounds are found to be not maintainable.
The ordinance simultaneously provided for a
review within a period of four months by the central
or the state government, as the case may be, and
thereafter further reviews at intervals not exceeding
four months. The scheme of the existing Act already
provides other safeguards such as that the central

government can review the orders of detention issued
by an officer of the central government or by a state
government or by any of its officers. Similarly, a
state government can review the orders of detention
issued by any of its officers.

This amendment follows the scheme of the ordinance
promulgated on June 29, 1975, for amending the
Maintenance of Internal Security Act, 1971.

A fresh ordinance

The central government promulgated yet another
ordinance on November 4, 1975, (which became law on
November 5), to provide for the forfeiture of illegally
acquired properties of smugglers and foreign exchange
racketeers.

The ordinance made it unlawful for any person to
whom it applies to hold any "illegally acquired
property, whether movable or immovable, either by
himself or through any other person on his behalf".
It is aimed at making sure that "big or habitual
offenders do not escape the clutches of the law",
according to an official handout.

The ordinance had covered four categories of
offenders. These are:
  1. Those convicted under the relevant laws for
     offences in relation to goods of value or
     amount in excess of Rs.1 lakh or those
     convicted more than once.
  2. People detained under the Conservation of
     Foreign Exchange and Prevention of Smuggling
     Activities Act, provided the detention order
     has not been set aside or revoked.
  3. Relatives of those in these two categories.
  4. Present holders of property previously held by
     persons in the first two categories, unless the
     present owner "was a transferee in good
     faith for adequate consideration".

The ordinance provided for the right of appeal
to a tribunal whose chairman shall be a person who is
qualified to be or has been a judge of the Supreme
Court or a High Court. The ordinance removes the
jurisdiction of civil courts from all matters connected
with this ordinance which are being handled by the
competent authority or the Appellate Tribunal. Thus
no injunction shall be granted by any court or any
other authority in respect of action taken under this
ordinance.

Codification

Some of these ordinances were codified into
statutes by the government. Most of these, however,
were later repealed, in the late 'seventies, with a
change in the government at the centre.

The importance of the spirit behind the ordinances

has, however, again been engaging the attention of
social reformers and economic analysts in the struggle
against smuggling and economic offences, and most of
these are likely to get back in the statutes of law,
after a comprehensive juristic appraisal, with
appropriate constitutional safeguards.

Annexure 4
MONETARY INDICATORS FOR THE
INDIAN ECONOMY

The latest monetary indicators for the national economy of India during October 1980, (as compared with the same in September 1980 and October 1979), have been compiled (Table A.4.1)from the statistical intelligence of the Department of Research and Statistics, Reserve Bank of India. This is relevant to the economic appraisal made earlier in this treatise in chapters 6 and 7.

Table A.4.1
Monetary indicators

Figures in crores of rupees

	October 1979	September 1980	October 1980
1. Notes in circulation	10,809	11,827	12,426
2. Notes issued	10,846	11,841	12,438
3. Foreign exchange assets (foreign securities plus balances held abroad)	5,186	4,811	4,661
4* Liabilities to the banking system (excluding borrowings from banks)	842	1,167	1,208
5* Liabilities to others (excluding borrowings)	32,714	37,058	37,805
6* Bank credit			
Loans, cash-credits and overdrafts	19,012	20,920	21,393
Bills (inland and foreign)	2,410	2,641	2,744
7. Money supply	23,257	23,415	22,599

* Relates to all scheduled banks.

Source:
   Compiled from the Statistical Supplement to the Reserve Bank of India Bulletin for week ending November 10 and 17, 1980.

Bibliography

BOOKS AND TREATISES

Anjaria
Price Control in India with Special Reference to Food Supply, 1946, Popular Book Depot, Bombay.

Appleby, P.H.
Policy and Administration, 1949, University of Alabama Press, U.S.A.

Ayres, C.E.
The Theory of Economic Progress, 1944, The University of North Carolina Press, U.S.A.

Baumel, W.J.
Economic Theory and Operations Analysis, 1963, Prentice Hall of India Ltd.

Bharatiya Vidya Bhavan
1. Indian History, British Period.
2. Indian History, Muslim Period.

Boulding, K.E.
1. A Reconstruction of Economics, 1950, John Wiley & Sons Inc., New York.
2. Economic Analysis, 1955, Hamish Hamilton, London.
3. The Economics of Peace, 1945, Prentice-Hall, Inc., New York.

Chamberlin, E.H.
Theory of Monopolistic Competition, 1962, Oxford University Press, London.

Clark, J.M.
Special Control of Business.

Clay, H.
Economics for the General Reader.

Cohen, R.L.
Economics of Agriculture, Cambridge Economic Handbook.

Cole, G.D.H.
Some Relations Between Political and Economic Theory, 1934, Macmillan and Co., London.

Commons, J.R.
The Economics of Collective Action, 1950, The Macmillan Company, London.

Cushman, R.E.
The Independent Regulatory Commissions, Oxford University Press, London.

178

Dalton, J.E.	Sugar: A Case Study of Government Control, 1937, The Macmillan Company London.
Das Gupta, A.K.	Planning and Economic Growth, 1965, George Allen and Unwin, London.
Dickinson, H.D.	Economics of Socialism, 1935, Oxford University Press, London.
Dimcock	Business and Government, 1949, Henry Holt and Co. Inc., New York.
Dobb, M.	Some Aspects of Economic Development: Three Lectures, Delhi School of Economics, Occasional Papers No.3.
Fleming, I.	Diamonds Are Forever.
Galbraith, J.K.	A Theory of Price Control, 1952, Harvard University Press, Cambridge.
Geoffrey, M.	Economic Development and the Price Level, 1950.
Ghosh, P.K.	Economic Controls in India, 1973, Vikas Publishing House, Delhi.
Graham, G.A.	Regulatory Administration, 1943, John Wiley & Sons, Inc., New York.
Hansen, A.H.	Principles of Political Economy, Macmillan and Company, London.
Herrman, L.F.	Agricultural Price Policy in India, 1966, Ministry of Food and Agriculture, New Delhi.
Irwin, R.	Readings in Price Theory, 1952, American Economic Association, Illinois, U.S.A.
Jacobson et al	Foundation Lectures on Monetary Policy and Fiscal Policy, 1965.
Jather and Beri	Indian Economics, Vol.1, 1949, Oxford University Press, Calcutta.
Kaldor, Nicholas.	Indian Tax Reforms.
Keezer, Dexter, Merriam and Associates.	Making Capitalism Work.
Keynes, J.M.	General Theory of Employment, Interest and Money, 1936, Macmillan and Company, London.
Khatkhate, D.R.	The Impact of Inflation on India's Economic Development, Asia Publishing House, Bombay.
Lerner, A.P.	Economics of Control.
Lewis, W.A.	The Theory of Economic Growth.
Madalgi, S.S.	Population and Food Supply in India, 1970, Lalvani Publishing House, Delhi.
Marshall, A.	Principles of Economics.
Mathew, E.T.	Agricultural Taxation and Economic Development in India, 1968, Asia Publishing House, Bombay.

Mazumdar, R.C.	Ancient India, 1949.
Mendes-France, P.	Economics and Action, 1955, William Heinemann, London.
NCAER	1. Savings in India During the Plan Periods, 1966, New Delhi. 2. Growth Without Inflation, 1956, New Delhi.
Nurkse R.	Problems of Capital Formation in Underdeveloped Countries, 1953, Oxford University Press, London.
Orton, W.	The Economic Role of the State, 1950, University of Chicago Press, U.S.A.
Pigou, A.C.	1. Economics of Unemployment. 2. Economics of Welfare. 3. Socialism Versus Capitalism.
Ranking, Peglar and Spicer	The Rights and Duties of Liquidators, Trustees and Receivers, 21st edition, Sir Issac Pitman and Sons Ltd., London.
Rather, A.W.	Planning Under Capitalism, 1935, P.S. King and Son Ltd., London.
Robinson, E.A.G.	Monopoly, Cambridge Economic Handbook.
Robinson, Joan	The Economics of Imperfect Competition.
Sahota, G.S.	Indian Tax Structure and Economic Development in India, 1961, Asia Publishing House, Bombay.
Samuelson, P.A.	1. Foundations of Economic Analysis. 2. Economics, An Introductory Analysis.
Shamasastry, R.	Kautilya's Arathashastra, 1956.
Singer, H.W.	Recent Trends in Economic Thought on Underdeveloped Countries, 1960.
Spicer and Peglar	Practical Auditing, 1961, Sir Issac Pitman and Sons Ltd., London.
Smith, A.	Inquiry Into the Nature and Causes of the Wealth of Nations, Cannan's Edition, 1904, Modern Library, London.
Steiner	Government's Role in Economic Life.
Stigler, G.J.	The Theory of Price.
Toynbee, A.J.	Civilisation on Trial.
Yutang, Lin.	The Wisdom of Confucius, 1939, Carlton House, Inc., New York.

ARTICLES AND PAPERS

Abel, M.E.	Agriculture in India in 1970, Economic and Political Weekly, (Review of Agriculture), May 1970.

Anjaria.   Reserve Bank of India Bulletin,
                            January 1969.

Ayub Syed.   Smugglers in the Net; What Now ?
                            The Illustrated Weekly of India,
                            November 1974.

Cole, G.D.H.   1. Socialisation, Encyclopaedia of
                               Social Science, London.
                            2. Laissez Faire, Encyclopaedia of
                               Social Science, London.

Dorrace, G.   Inflation and Growth, The Statisti-
                            cal Evidence, I.M.F. Staff Press,
                            March 1968.

Gupta, P.D.   Black Market, Further Consideration,
                            Yojana, March 14, 1965.

Hunder, M.H.   Business in Government, Opinion and
                            Comment, November 23, 1943.

Kalechi.   The Principles of Economic Risk,
                            Economica, November 1937.

Lester, R.A.   Political Economy Vs Individualistic
                            Economics, American Economic Review,
                            Vol. 28, No.1, March 1938.

Mukherjee, Aruna.   Smuggling, The Indian Express,
                            New Delhi, September 29, 1974.

Plumtre, A.F.W.   The Theory of Black Market, Further
                            Considerations, Canadian Journal of
                            Economics and Political Science,
                            Vol. 13, No.2, May 1974.

Ray, S.K.   Inflation and Growth, Business
                            Standard, Calcutta, January 10 & 11,
                            1980.
                            Inflation As An Economic Phenomenon,
                            Financial Express, Bombay, June 28
                            & 29, 1979.
                            Extent of Corruption in Economy,
                            The Hindu, Madras, June 25, 1979.
                            Management Audit, Management
                            Accountant, Calcutta, May 1979.
                            The Parallel Economic Structure,
                            Business Standard, Calcutta,
                            January 6, 8 & 9, 1979.
                            Financing For Development, Business
                            Standard, Calcutta, November 20 &
                            21, 1978.
                            Black Marketing: Further Considera-
                            tions, Economic Times, Bombay,
                            October 10 & 11, 1978.
                            Smuggling Network, Economic Times,
                            Bombay, June 24 & 25, 1978.
                            Emergence & Proliferation of Black
                            Money, Economic Times, Bombay,
                            May 3 & 4, 1978.

	India's Balance of Payments, Business Standard, Calcutta, March 4 & 6, 1978. Disequilibrium Today, Business Standard, Calcutta, July 19, 1977. The Profiteering Curve, Financial Express, Bombay, May 9, 1977. This Inflationary Decade. Business Standard, Calcutta, April 18 & 19, 1977. Profiteering, An Economic Analysis, Eastern Economist, New Delhi, October 20, 1975. Recent Trends in Fundamental Economics, Eastern Economist, New Delhi, August 15, 1975.
Shah, M.	Hunt for Black Money, Commerce, August 19, 1967.
Stafford, J.	Indices of Wholesale Prices, Journal of the Royal Statistical Society, (Series A), Part IV, 1951.
Vakil, C.N.	1. Measures To Check The Growth of Unrecorded Gain, Supplement to Capital, December 24, 2. Liquidity in the Indian Economy, Reserve Bank of India Bulletin, November, 1963.
Valayudhan	1. Reserve Bank of India Bulletin, June 1967. 2. Reserve Bank of India Bulletin, January 1969.

REPORTS AND DOCUMENTS [1]

Annual Reports on Currency and Finance, Reserve Bank of India.
Annual Economic Surveys, Ministry of Finance, Government of India.
Bulletins on Food Statistics, Ministry of Food and Agriculture.
Census of India Reports.
Commentary on Corruption, A Survey By the Indian Institute of Public Opinion, 1972.
Economic Survey and General Budget Papers, 1974.
Economic Survey and General Budget Papers, 1975.
Final Report of Direct Taxes Enquiry Committee, 1971.
Fair Price for Sugar, Tariff Commission, Bombay, 1969.
Final Report of the Committee on Prevention of Corruption.
Final Report on Rationalisation and Simplification of the Tax Structure, Government of India.
Five Year Plans, Planning Commission, Government of India.

182

Approach Papers and Mid-Term Appraisals of Five Year
Plans, Planning Commission, Government of India.
Income Tax Enquiry Report, 1936.
Index Number of Wholesale Prices in India, Revised
Series, Week ending April 14, 1956, Government of India.
Interim Report of the Direct Taxes Enquiry Committee,
1970.
Indian Tax Reform, Report of a Survey by Nicholas Kaldor.
Indian Labour Statistics.
Report of the Administrative Reforms Commission on
Central Direct Taxes Administration.
Report of the Agricultural Prices Commission.
Report of Comptroller and Auditor General of India,
1969-70.
Report of the Direct Taxes Administration Enquiry
Committee, 1958-59.
Report on the Drug Industry by a sub-panel of the
Hathi Committee.
Report of the Foodgrains Enquiry Committee, November
1957.
Report of Foodgrains Policy Committee, 1968.
Report on a Framework for Incomes and Prices Policy,
Reserve Bank of India, 1967.
Report of the Fifth Finance Commission, 1969.
Reports on Minimum Prices for Wheat and Gram for
the 1968-69 Crop.
Report on Minimum Support Prices for Rabi Foodgrains,
1969-70.
Report of Indian Toxicological Research Centre, 1975.
Reports on Price Policy for Kharif Cereals.
Reports on Price Policy for Rabi Foodgrains.
Report of the Sugar Enquiry Commission, October 1965.
Report of the Study Team of the Administrative Reforms
Commission on Promotion Policies, Conduct Rules, Discipl-
ine and Morale.
Report of the Taxation Enquiry Commission, 1953-54.
Some Basic Statistics Relating to the Indian Economy,
Supplement to Reserve Bank of India Bulletin, 1971 to
1974.
The Reform Planning, Report of the Expert Group,
Department of Economic and Social Affairs, United Nations,
New York, 1971.
Economic Development with Stability, Ministry of
Finance, Government of India, 1954.

ACTS, ORDINANCES AND LAW CASES[2]

Indian Penal Code, 45 of 1860.
Indian Trusts Act, VI of 1882.
Kingston Cotton Mills Case, No.2, 1896.
Rex V. Kylsant and Morland, 1931, Accountant, 1931, LR.
The Westminister Road Constructions & Engineering Co.Ltd.
Case, 1932, (Accountant, February 1932, p.203 to 204).

Pendlebury's Ltd. V. Eills Green & Co., 1936, 80 Acct.
L.R. 39.
Insolvency Act, Act V of 1920.
Prevention of Food Adulteration Act, 1954, amended upto
1975.
Delhi Rent Control Act, 1958.
The Income Tax Act, 1961.
Conservation of Foreign Exchange and Prevention of
Smuggling Activities Act, 1974, No.52 of 1974.
Taxation Laws Amendment Act, 1975.
Concessional Tax Ordinance, 1975.
Anti-Smuggling Ordinance, December 1975.
Maintenance of Internal Security Act.
Disciplinary Action and Appeal Rules and Fundamental
Rules for Central and State Government Establishments
in India.
Hand Book of Civil Service Laws and Practices, United
Nations.

NOTES

1. These references have been arranged in order of
their appearance in the text of the treatise. Some of
the references, however, appear more than once.
2. Ibid.

Index

Printed in the United States
by Baker & Taylor Publisher Services